Understanding
Research Methods
in Psychology

Understanding Research Methods in Psychology

Jennie Brooks Jamison, M.Ed.

Worth Publishers

Publisher: Catherine Woods

Acquisitions Editor: Erik Gilg

Development Editor: Jaclyn Castaldo

Marketing Manager: Cindy Weiss

Senior Designer, Cover Designer: Lee Ann McKevitt

Associate Managing Editor: Tracey Kuehn

Project Editor: Laura McGinn

Production Manager: Sarah Segal

Composition: Northeastern Graphic, Inc.

Printing and Binding: RR Donnelley

"International Baccalaureate" is a registered trademark of the International Baccalaureate Organization (IB). The material in this text has been developed independently of the IB, which was not involved in the production of this text and in no way endorses it.

AP is a registered trademark and/or owned by the College Board, which was not involved in the production of, and does not endorse, this product.

ISBN-13: 978-1-4292-6191-3

ISBN-10: 1-4292-6191-9

Printed in the United States of America

Third printing

Worth Publishers

41 Madison Avenue

New York, NY 10010

www.worthpublishers.com

About the Author

Jennie Brooks Jamison, M.Ed., has been teaching International Baccalaureate (IB) psychology since 1986 at St. Petersburg High School in Florida. Jennie leads workshops for IB psychology and is an experienced examiner for the internal assessment project and external exams. Jennie's first publication with Worth, *Levels of Analysis in Psychology: A Companion Reader for Use with the IB Psychology Course,* was published in 2010. Jennie lives in St. Petersburg, Florida, with her husband and three cats.

For my father, John Brooks
Fifty years of teaching is inspiring.

Contents

1

Introduction   1

A Framework for Understanding the Different Research Methods ■ The Problem-Solving Process in Psychology ■ Distinguish Between Qualitative and Quantitative Data ■ Explain Strengths and Limitations of a Qualitative Approach to Research

2

Sampling in Quantitative and Qualitative Research 10

Representative Sampling ■ Non-representative Sampling ■ Discuss Sampling Techniques Appropriate to Qualitative Research

3

Ethics in Quantitative and Qualitative Research   16

Context for Thinking about Ethics ■ Discuss Ethical Considerations in Qualitative Research

4

Triangulation   21

Introduction to the Concept of Triangulation

Observation ■ Discuss How Researchers Analyze Data Obtained in
Observational Research

8

Case Studies: Qualitative Approach 60

Introduction to Case Studies ■ Case Study 1: A Case Study about
Families Receiving Eating Disorder Treatment Using a Multiple Case
Study Design ■ Case Study 2: A Case Study about Emotions and Sport
Performance ■ Evaluate the Use of Case Studies in Research ■
Discuss the Extent to Which Findings Can Be Generalized from a
Single Case Study ■ Explain How a Case Study Could Be Used to
Investigate A Problem in an Organization or Group

9

Questionnaires: Quantitative Approach 69

Genetics and Cross-Cultural Research Are Two Places Where Students
Encounter Questionnaires—Introduction to Questionnaires ■
Questionnaire Study 1: Use of the EAT-26 Questionnaire in a Field
Experiment about Attitudes toward Disordered Eating ■ Questionnaire
Study 2: Use of the Diagnostic Interview Schedule (DIS-IV) Questionnaire
in a Correlation Study about Depression ■ Questionnaire Study 3: Use of
the Singelis Self-Construal Scale in a Correlation Study about How Culture
Affects the Brain ■ Should Questionnaires Use Open-Ended or Closed-
Ended Response Scales? ■ Sampling for Quantitative Studies Using
Questionnaires ■ Standardizing Questionnaires ■ Evaluating Data from
Questionnaires ■ Interpreting Correlations ■ Advantages and
Disadvantages of Using Questionnaires

10

Designing an Experiment 84

Some Context for Experimentation ■ Characteristics of Experiments ■
Conducting Experimental Research ■ Introduction ■ Aim of the Study
■ Literature Review ■ Research Hypothesis ■ Null Hypothesis ■
Method ■ Design ■ Ethics in Experiments ■ Participants ■ Materials
■ Ideas for Designing Materials ■ Procedures

11

Analyzing Data from an Experiment   105

Some Context for Thinking about Data Analysis ■ Level of Measurement ■ Results ■ Descriptive Statistics ■ Inferential Statistics ■ Discussion ■ Generalizing from Experiments

Preface

I am convinced that my teaching is useful to students only if it accomplishes two goals. Students must really understand the material and should be able to apply the information to their own lives.

Psychology is always evolving, and this book reflects research methods used in modern psychology. What is valued as knowledge changes over time, and students need to tolerate the uncertainty that comes with the natural fluidity and growth of knowledge.

What counts as knowledge in psychology? Over time, the answer to this question has changed. While quantitative research, such as experiments and correlation studies, makes up much of what students study in their first psychology course, there has recently been an explosion of interest in qualitative research methods. In addition, there is a growing interest in the concept of triangulation.

Students of modern psychology need to understand both quantitative and qualitative research methods. Each type of research method is valuable and has a specific purpose. Research from both quantitative and qualitative studies helps us understand the full complexities of the human experience.

As a longtime educator, I have talked with hundreds of teachers, all facing the same dilemma. How do we push students to cognitively advance in a short period of time, typically before they advance on their own? Students tend to revert to memorizing whenever they face new material. Memorizing is inefficient, and I constantly address its shortcomings. I see that students easily remember the facts, but the meaning of the facts is too often missing. Memorizing is especially problematic when learning about research methods because they are tools used to understand behavior rather than specific things.

Most high school students are just developing sophisticated cognitive abilities and consider research methods abstractions. I like to reframe this idea by telling students that the facts are the abstractions and are meaningless outside understanding how the facts are known. It is my job as a teacher to push students beyond their current capabilities so that they are better equipped to navigate the world. It helps if students have the chance to conduct their own studies using a variety of methods. For example, students typically do not understand the strengths and limitations of experiments until they design and run their own. Students tend to call all research an "experiment" and do not see differences between the different research methods until they run their own studies.

This Book's Three Purposes

This book has three purposes.

One purpose is to help students see that there are many options available to researchers for investigating behavior and that each method has a specific goal.

The second purpose is to introduce students to qualitative research methods: interviewing, observation, and case studies. International Baccalaureate (IB) students taking the Higher Level (HL) course sit for Paper 3, a section of the exam about qualitative research. I weave headings throughout the chapters on qualitative research that correspond to Paper 3 learning outcomes. These IB learning outcomes are relevant for any psychology student.

The third purpose is to teach students how to design a simple experiment and analyze the data.

Students taking the International Baccalaureate and/or Advanced Placement exams in psychology will find what they need in this book. Research methods are probably the most difficult part of these exams. Introductory texts do not usually provide enough depth, while the typical college-level research methods books are too complicated, sometimes even for a college student's first experience with methodology.

Acknowledgments

I want to thank everyone at Worth Publishers for their support, including Erik Gilg for sponsoring the book, Jaclyn Castaldo for her advice as the development editor, Cindi Weiss for marketing it, Laura McGinn for managing the project, and Karen Osborne for the valuable copyediting feedback.

Introduction

A Framework for Understanding the Different Research Methods

"I want to understand why people behave the way they do." This is the most common reason students give for signing up for my psychology course. At the beginning of the class, I find that students know little about the kinds of questions psychologists investigate. Rather, most students have a "lay" understanding of psychology based on common wisdom, stereotypes, and anecdotes.

The answers to questions about why people behave the way they do are actually complicated. Human behavior is complex, and there is no one explanation for it. In fact, any behavior is the result of numerous contributing factors. Modern psychologists take a level-of-analysis approach to understanding all the factors that go into creating and maintaining human behavior.

Genes contribute to behavior, but there are also numerous cognitive, social learning, and cultural factors that interact with genes to create and maintain behavior in ways we are just beginning to understand. Over time and contrary to popular belief, rather than narrowing down causes of behavior, modern research has shown how complex it really is and acknowledges that we still have a lot to learn. We are less certain about the causes of behavior now, but the answers are more realistic.

In order to know about behavior, researchers must tackle the task of pulling apart all the factors contributing to behavior. Modern researchers often try to see how some of the different factors relate to each other in one study.

There are two general approaches to research, **quantitative** and **qualitative.** Much of the research in a high school course is quantitative, such as experiments and studies gathering data with questionnaires and analyzing it with correlations. However, the field of qualitative research has grown significantly since the mid-1990s and offers researchers ways of understanding behavior not possible with quantitative methods. Qualitative methods include case studies, some types of interviewing, and observation.

Students studying modern psychology should understand both approaches.

The Problem-Solving Process in Psychology

Psychologists go through a problem-solving process any time they create research questions about human behavior; when a researcher sees a problem, the researcher creates a research question to investigate it. Here are some examples of research questions:

1. Does watching violent media cause aggression?
2. Which treatments work for treating depression?
3. Why do male and female mathematical skills differ?
4. What are the prevalence rates of mental illness around the world?
5. Does the concept "disordered eating" differ by culture?
6. How might a polymorphism (gene variation) interact with environmental factors to increase one's risk of depression?
7. Does living in different cultures (individualistic or collectivist) modify neural structures?
8. Do people from different cultures comply with requests the same way?
9. How do boys view their body image?
10. How might one's culture affect how one views depressive symptoms and their appropriate treatment?
11. How do individuals make meaning of their recovery experience from alcohol addiction?
12. To what extent can doctors accurately tell if someone has a mental illness?
13. How do children use stories to help them understand cultural expectations?

14. How can we understand the progress of patients in their treatment for an eating disorder?

15. How can we maximize an athlete's sport performance?

It is a good thing that there is more than one research method because these questions ask a variety of things. Each method serves a different purpose, and *the different methods are selected depending on what we want to know about behavior.* Just one method would not give us a comprehensive picture of behavior.

Here is a list of the research methods selected to tackle the example research questions. **Some of these studies are reviewed in depth in this book.** Some of the studies not reviewed in this book are free on the Internet.

1. Bandura (1965; Bandura, Ross, & Ross, 1963) used controlled lab experiments for the classic series of Bobo doll experiments to demonstrate that the modeling of media is an important cause of aggressive behavior.

2. Keller and colleagues (2008), DeRubeis and colleagues (2005), Babyak and colleagues (2000), Christensen and Burrows (1990), and Qi Guijun and Sang Peng in 2005 (Wolfe, 2005) all used experiments to investigate the efficacy of different depression treatments, and all the treatments were beneficial to participants. The treatments were the combination of drugs and cognitive therapy, cognitive therapy alone for severe depression, exercise, diet change, and acupuncture.

3. Kimura and Clarke (2002) designed a quasi-experiment to investigate differences in male and female cognitive mapping skills.

4. The World Health Organization (2004) ran a survey to investigate the prevalence of mental illness worldwide.

5. Becker, Burwell, Gilman, Herzog, and Hamburg (2002) studied disordered eating in Fijian adolescent females before and after the widespread availability of television. They collected data in two ways, with a field experiment and with an interview. The field experiment data were analyzed with correlations, and the interviews were analyzed with content analysis. The questionaires part of the Becker study is detailed in Chapter 9 and the interviews part in Chapter 6.

6. Caspi and colleagues (2003) used questionnaires to measure the amount of depression and the number of stressful events in a sample and correlated these findings with an individual's genotype for the serotonin transporter gene in a gene–environment correlation study. The Caspi study is detailed in Chapter 9.

7. Chiao and colleagues (2009) used a questionnaire to classify people as either collectivist or individualist and then used fMRI to see if the neural structures of the two groups differed. The Chiao study is detailed in Chapter 9. *biological*
Sociocultural

8. Petrova, Cialdini, and Sills (2007) used email interviews to see if compliance was similar across cultures. Data were analyzed with correlations.

9. Hargreaves and Tiggermann (2006) used focus group interviews to investigate boys' body image. The Hargraves and Tiggemann study is detailed in Chapter 6.

10. Okello and Musisi (2006) used focus group interviews to investigate how cultural views of the Baganda of Uganda shaped the way they viewed depressive symptoms and appropriate treatment. The Okello and Musisi study is detailed in Chapter 6.

11. Ehrmin (2002) used overt participant-observation to study substance-dependent recovery experiences of African-American women. Ehrmin also interviewed the women. The Ehrmin study is detailed in Chapter 7.

12. Rosenhan (1973) used covert participant-observation to study whether or not doctors could tell if someone had a mental disorder. The Rosenhan study is detailed in Chapter 7.

13. Alexander, Miller, and Hengst (2001) used narrative interviews and diary-observations to collect data on how children's emotional attachments to stories help them make meaning in their culture. Content analysis was selected to analyze data. The Alexander study is detailed in Chapter 7.

14. Ma (2008) used a case study to identify themes emerging from family therapy for eating disorders. The Ma study is detailed in Chapter 8.

15. Cohen, Tenenbaum, and English (2006) used a case study to document the unique zone of optimal emotional arousal for two athletes and showed how they benefited from training to hit their peak performance within this zone. The Cohen study is detailed in Chapter 8.

Distinguish between Qualitative and Quantitative Data

The goals of research dictate whether a psychologist uses quantitative or qualitative research methods. Researchers using **quantitative methods** seek objective knowledge and gather data with numbers. In contrast, researchers using **qualitative methods** seek meaning and context and do not quantify human characteristics.

Note to IB Students

Students must go into the study of quantitative and qualitative research methods understanding that many research design concepts, such as representation from sampling, the role of the researcher as objective, triangulation, internal validity (relating to credibility), and generalizing (related to external validity), were first formulated for quantitative methods. Rethinking the meaning of these concepts is crucial for interpreting qualitative studies. *This means that research concepts have different meanings when applied to qualitative studies.*

One might automatically think of the quantitative use of research design concepts when they think about qualitative methods. A student must not do this! This is probably going to be the hardest thing for students. This is a good place to practice tolerating uncertainty.

The concepts of quantitative research methods were influenced by **positivism, empiricism,** and **hypothetico-deductivism.** A positivist approach means "that the goal of research is to produce objective knowledge" (Willig, 2001, p. 3). Empiricism means that knowledge of the world must come from direct observations (induction), not from something abstract (deduction) (Snape & Spencer, 2003). Hypothetico-deductivism means that theories are generated and then tested in a process called **falsification.** Quantitative scientific methods stem from the idea that scientists create theories and then test the theories (often in controlled lab experiments) to see if they can be falsified. If the theories cannot be falsified, then they have support (not proof). Supporters of qualitative methods critique quantitative methods for the general reason that "there are no fixed or overarching meanings because meanings are a product of time and place" (Snape & Spencer, 2003, p. 9). Researchers using qualitative methods prefer to study people in real-life situations.

In quantitative research methods, data are gathered and analyzed in numerical form. For example, all experiments use quantitative methods. In addition, surveys and questionnaires are also frequently quantified, often using **Likert Scales** to gather data, where answers may fall into a range from "strongly agree" to "strongly disagree."

According to Hugh Coolican (2004), quantitative methods have seven qualities:

1. They are intended to be narrow and focused.
2. They are objective.
3. They are intended to be artificial.

6

4. They are highly structured.

5. They are not meant to show the context of real life, meaning that the studies have low ecological validity. This means that the conditions of the study do not generalize well to real-life situations.

6. They are reliable.

7. They are low in reflexivity, meaning that the researcher intends to stay objective and does not reflect on how he or she might have influenced the results.

Quantitative data are a suitable choice for certain kinds of research questions.

For example, the *only* way to answer research questions about causation is to run an experiment. In lab experiments, researchers have the ability to control all factors that might influence how an independent variable affects a dependent variable. Bandura's Bobo doll experiments are examples. Another example is studying mental and physical health treatments. Establishing causation is required for showing that treatments are effective.

A second research example is set up when a researcher wants to know the relationship (correlation) between two or more variables. One example is studying the relationship between genes and stressful lives. Caspi and colleagues (2003) used two questionnaires to correlate stressful life events and depressive symptoms to having genetic variations of the serotonin transporter gene.

In contrast, qualitative research does not use numerical values (other than some percentages or frequencies that are then used to generate themes) and is very different from quantitative research. *Be aware that there is no one accepted way to design qualitative research,* so you will see a lot of variety in study designs.

The seven qualities of qualitative research are the opposite of quantitative methods (Coolican, 2004):

1. They provide a rich range of information rather than narrowly focused information.

2. They are subjective.

3. They reflect the natural environment of behavior, the opposite of artificiality.

4. They are loosely structured and sometimes unstructured.

5. They have ecological validity.

6. They have low reliability.

7. They are high in reflexivity.

Dawn Snape and Liz Spencer (2003) add more to defining qualitative methods:

1. A qualitative method is an **emic approach to understanding behavior**. Emic approaches delve into the unique perspective of individuals and/or groups, sometimes challenging the assumed etics, or universal behaviors, that researchers often have about people at the beginning of a research study.

2. It is meant to study context, meaning, and processes characterizing behavior.

3. Its research strategies are flexible and are conducted in the real world.

4. Data collection is supposed to be sensitive to the context of the person.

5. There tends to be close contact between researchers and participants.

6. Much of the data analysis is aimed at identifying themes/categories that emerge from the data.

Several objections to quantitative research led to the development and growing acceptance of qualitative methods (Coolican, 2004):

1. Quantitative methods ignore the context of the person and often separate out a section of behavior, such as "memory," from the rest of the person.

2. Even if researchers think they are objective, their impersonal relationship with study participants might influence the outcome of the study.

3. Experiments and questionnaires gather superficial information. The context is typically ignored. For example, the EAT-26, a commonly used questionnaire to assess a person's level of disordered eating, does not gather information about the person's social context. The answers to the questions may be the result of social conditions or cultural rules, and the risk to participants is that they can be wrongly categorized as "at high risk for developing an eating disorder" when the preoccupation with food might be simply the result of living in an impoverished country.

Sometimes qualitative research is the *only* way a topic can be studied. For example, how else would we know about personal experiences with addiction recovery?

Researchers frequently combine quantitative and qualitative methods. For example, Becker and colleagues' (2002) research about disordered eating in Fijian adolescents was partially a field experiment and partially an interview study.

Sometimes more than one qualitative method is used in a single study. Alexander and colleagues (2001) used narrative interviews and self-observation diaries to study children's language use. Ehrmin (2002) used participant-observation and interviews to study addiction recovery. In each study, the two methods complemented each other.

Since the 1990s, qualitative methods have seen an "explosion of interest" and have become more accepted as valid research (Snape & Spencer, 2003, p. 10). Before the mid-1990s, there was some use of qualitative methods. Cultural psychology is a good example. Cultural psychologists had a tradition of using ethnography (observations of cultural practices), which was borrowed from anthropology. Now qualitative methods are used to study a wide range of behaviors.

Explain Strengths and Limitations of a Qualitative Approach to Research

Strengths of qualitative research methods include the following:

1. If the goal is to study the context of a person—how a person makes meaning of a situation or documents a process—then qualitative methods are the best choice.

2. To build on strength 1, sometimes qualitative methods are the *only* way we can study behavior. For example, the only way for Becker and colleagues (2002) to understand the thoughts and feelings of Fijian adolescent girls about disordered eating was to interview a subgroup from the original sample that took the EAT-26 questionnaire. The researchers were interested in the themes that emerged from the interviews from a group representing different degrees of disordered eating. They were the first people to study disordered eating in Fiji. The themes that emerged helped psychologists understand one result of rapid cultural change on behavior. As another example, V. S. Ramachandran (Ritsko & Rawlence, 2001) showed that Freud's theory of the Oedipal complex was incorrect through his study of David, who suffered from Capgras syndrome. (David thought his parents were imposters after he had an accident in which he received a head injury. Fortunately, David's brain repaired itself over time.) We have

to wait for the unfortunate results of accidents to observe these types of cases. Cases such as David's give neurologists the chance to develop new hypotheses about the brain and behavior.

3. Qualitative methods address the limitations of quantitative methods.
4. Qualitative methods are important for **triangulation,** addressed in Chapter 4.

Limitations of qualitative methods include the following:

1. They are uncontrolled and hard to replicate. time.
2. They have low population validity, one type of external validity.

However, these limitations are somewhat superficial. *We should not criticize research for meeting its goals.* It is similar to criticizing experiments for being too artificial and lacking ecological validity. Experiments are supposed to be and must be artificial to show a clear cause and effect. In the same way, qualitative methods are supposed to portray the context of participants.

Sampling in Quantitative and Qualitative Research

There are two general types of sampling: **representative** (probability) and **nonrepresentative** (nonprobability).

Representative Sampling

Representative sampling means identifying a **target population,** the group you wish to generalize your findings to, and selecting a subsample that represents that target population. Representative sampling is useful when a researcher wants to generalize the findings to a larger group or when the sample is an estimate of the incidence of something, such as the prevalence of a behavior (Ritchie, Lewis, & Elam, 2003). The whole point of sampling is to make data gathering manageable. It is usually impossible to study an entire target population, so we take a smaller sample of this larger target population.

Two examples of representative sampling are **simple random sampling** and **stratified random sampling.** Representative samples are most appropriate for quantitative studies. But contrary to popular belief, representative sampling is not as widely used as you might expect.

Simple random sampling means that everyone in the target population has an equal chance of being selected for the sample. A random sample is best selected by first assigning everyone in the target population a number, then generating random numbers with a calculator or computer. For example, if I want to generalize the findings of an experiment to all of the 11th-grade IB students at St. Petersburg High School, I would assign each junior a number between 1 and perhaps 130. Then I would program my calculator or computer to randomly select numbers between 1 and 130 until my sample is selected, perhaps 30 students.

Stratified random sampling means that a target population is divided into subcategories, where each subcategory represents a proportion of the total population. If IB students make up 25% of St. Petersburg High School, then 25% of a stratified sample of St. Petersburg High School must be IB students. This is a very time-consuming process, but the advantage is that the sample really represents the total makeup of the school.

Representative sampling is the only kind of sampling that allows for the statistical generalization of study results outside the sample.

Qualitative studies typically do not use representative samples, and students must accept that the concept "representational" has a different meaning when generalizing from qualitative data. Chapter 5 includes a detailed discussion of generalizing from qualitative research.

While random sampling is the best kind of sampling to use to generalize findings outside a sample, it is in fact rarely used, even in experiments. Most experiments use opportunity samples, such as the students in an introductory psychology course at a university. Sometimes students think that efficacy studies of mental health treatment use random samples. However, many of these studies are opportunity samples of patients in clinics who meet specific exclusion criteria. Statisticians prefer random samples, but they are just too hard to put together in most cases. Triangulation takes care of generalizing from studies using nonrepresentative sampling; it addresses whether the findings from one study fit with the findings from a larger body of research.

Nonrepresentative Sampling

Three types of nonrepresentative sampling are opportunity sampling, purposive sampling, and theoretical sampling.

Nonrepresentative sampling does not necessarily represent a target population, but it *may* represent the target population. Statistically, the results of studies using nonrepresentative samples are generalizable only to the individuals studied. However, Chapter 5 includes a discussion about symbolic generalization, something it is possible to do from nonrepresentative samples in qualitative studies.

Jane Ritchie and colleagues (2003) make it clear that *qualitative research is not meant to be representative of a larger target population and representative means something a little different for qualitative research*. When using a non-representative sample, "units are deliberately selected to reflect particular features of or groups within the sampled population" (p. 78).

Be careful of criticizing studies for doing what they are supposed to do, including using sampling techniques that meet specific research goals.

Sampling Techniques Appropriate to Qualitative Research

Let's look more closely at opportunity sampling, purposive sampling, and theoretical sampling one at a time.

Opportunity sampling is appropriate to use for some types of qualitative research, but an opportunity sample is not rigorously selected; purposive sampling is far more rigorous. Sometimes students confuse the terms *opportunity sampling* and *convenience sampling*. Do these words mean the same thing? It depends on the source. Coolican (2004) uses the words as synonyms. Convenience/opportunity samples are made up of the participants who are most available, or convenient, to the researcher, such as an introductory psychology class, and provide an opportunity to conduct research. In contrast, Ritchie and colleagues (2003) think that the terms *opportunity sampling* and *convenience sampling* are different. Opportunity sampling means that a psychologist discovers chances to test ideas while conducting fieldwork and takes advantage of these chances as they arise. Convenience sampling means not having any specific sampling strategy and using participants who are convenient at the time. However, I do not want to create a big issue about this distinction. I will consider the terms synonyms and use the term *opportunity sampling* in this book.

Sometimes opportunity sampling is the best choice for a qualitative study. For example, Ehrmin (2002) used opportunity sampling in her combination observation/interview study to investigate the process of recovery from substance abuse in African-American women. Ehrmin spent three years studying the environmental context of women living in a transitional inner-city home for persons recovering from substance abuse.

The main strength of opportunity sampling is its ease. Its main limitation is that participants are not selected with any rigor; they have no specific characteristics that make them statistically representative of a larger group. They *may* represent a larger group, but you cannot be sure.

While opportunity sampling is used with some qualitative research, **purposive sampling** is more rigorous and is used more frequently. Purposive sampling means that the researcher selects a sample for a particular purpose: Participants have particular characteristics. Ritchie and colleagues (2003) use the term **symbolic representation** when referring to purposive samples. A sample is meant to symbolize a larger group, although technically it does not represent a target population the way that a representative sample does.

As an example, Becker, Burwell, Gilman, and Herzog (2002) used a study population of all the ethnic teenage girls from two high schools in Nadroga, Fiji. All participants filled out the EAT-26 questionnaire to assess disordered eating before and after television became widely available. After the field experiment, Becker and colleagues selected a purposive sample from the questionnaire sample. Interviews were collected "from a subset of 30 purposively sampled respondents with a range of disordered eating attitudes and behaviors and television viewing habits within the original sample" (p. 510).

Becker and colleagues did the things that Ritchie and colleagues (2003) outlined for selecting a good purposive sample.

1. They used a small sample that met the criteria for proper **sample coverage** (showed different points of view) of the topic for investigation. Small samples are typical in qualitative research for several reasons. First, there quickly comes a point in conducting qualitative research when the use of more participants adds nothing new to the analysis—*the study becomes saturated*. One notation of an opinion or attitude is enough to make a point of view part of the analysis. Second, there is no need for the sample to be representative of a situational context. Third, qualitative studies are rich in detail, and too many participants make the study unmanageable. How can a researcher provide a rich view of meaning and context if there are large numbers of participants?

2. Their **sample frame**, or information source, was well selected. Sample frames can come from different kinds of sources, such as administrative records, previously surveyed samples, a household screen (where interviews are conducted with all the households in a study area), or **snowball samples** (though it is a potential problem if the researcher does not give a specific criteria for the selection of the next participant in the snowball chain). Becker and colleagues used a previously surveyed sample for her purposive sample.

Coolican (2004) identifies several types of purposive sampling that fit the needs of qualitative research.

14

1. **Focus groups**. Focus groups are often made up of experts on a topic or people selected because they have certain experiences in common with one another.

2. **Snowball sampling**. Snowball sampling means to ask one expert for an interview, and then that person suggests the next expert participant, and so on. Robert Rosenthal (1993) used snowball sampling to study homeless people living in Santa Barbara, California. He did not have any contacts of his own to start the interviewing process, so he attended a meeting for the homeless. There he met a woman who introduced him to other homeless people. This is how Rosenthal gained entry into the lives of the homeless. Interestingly, Rosenthal experienced one limitation of snowball sampling. It is possible that when one person suggests other people for the sample, the people suggested represent only the point of view of the original interviewee. Rosenthal noticed that many of the tougher homeless people did not socialize with this woman and wondered if he had sampled the full range of opinion. It is important that researchers using snowball samples understand this potential problem and try to gain access to a variety of opinions and circumstances.

3. **Critical cases**. According to Coolican (2004), "a special case may sometimes highlight things that can be related back to most non-special cases" (p. 43).

In each type of purposive sample, the researcher must identify the sample frame (Ritchie et al., 2003). The sample frame is a series of decisions about the specific characteristics of participants. Characteristics could include a particular age group, one or both genders, people undergoing a specific type of mental or physical health treatment, people with different types or degrees of mental or physical health problems, people living in a specific type of neighborhood, or people representing specific attitudes. The psychologist must prioritize these characteristics so that the list does not get too long. Next, a **sample matrix** might be used to sort through all of the characteristics that should be included in the sample. For example, a sample matrix that is appropriate for a study on disordered eating can include four girls who watch a minimal amount of television and have a small amount of disordered eating, four girls who watch a large amount of television and have a high score for disordered eating, and so on.

The details of the sample characteristics in a purposive sample make it easier for independent critics to examine the proper **generalizing** from the study sample.

I include **theoretical sampling** because it is one way to get a sample for observation studies (Neuman, 2006). Theoretical sampling is really a type of purposive sampling where what is sampled is "guided by developing theory. . . . Field researchers sample times, situations, types of events, locations, types of people, or contexts of interest" (p. 406). Sampling evolves with the interpretation of field notes. For example, one sampling of a particular location might lead the researcher to ask questions that lead to new ideas about other locations and people to sample. Theoretical sampling is related to the term **grounded theory**, meaning that theory is created from interpreting each new set of data collected in a study. Not all observation studies use theoretical sampling. In fact, Ehrmin (2002) used opportunity sampling. But if a researcher is in the field and has the opportunity to study a variety of data, then theoretical sampling probably is a good choice.

Ethics in Quantitative and Qualitative Research

Context for Thinking about Ethics

It is expected that all ethical issues be resolved before research begins. Students living in particular regions should consult their country's guidelines. One example is the U.S. American Psychological Association (APA) guidelines, available from www.apa.org.

Many of the same ethical considerations apply to both experimental and nonexperimental research. I will discuss ethical issues critical to running experiments in Chapter 10. The issues discussed in this chapter are important for qualitative research and also apply to quantitative nonexperimental research.

Discuss Ethical Considerations in Qualitative Research

Jane Lewis (2003) identifies four ethical concerns relevant to the unstructured features of qualitative research.

1. Informed consent from all participants is required.
2. Anonymity and confidentiality are guaranteed.
3. Participants are protected from potential harm.
4. Researchers are protected from potential harm.

I add three ethical issues specific to observation studies.

a. Psychologists using participant-observation may not want participants to know about the study. This means that careful thought must go into the planning stages. Bill Gillham (2008) writes that the debate is complicated because of the difference between covert observations (people do not know they are being observed) and overt observations (people know they are being observed). In addition, some observations take place in open settings (public places) and some take place in closed settings (such as a classroom). Considering the ethics of an observation study requires knowledge of all four (covert, overt, open, closed). For example, a study could be overt and in a closed setting, such as Ehrmin's (2002). Or a study could be covert and in a closed setting, such as Rosenhan's (1973). The way a study is set up drives the discussion about getting or not getting informed consent.

b. Gillham (2008) asks the question who owns the observations? Do participants in **ethnography** have the right to go back and challenge what is recorded and how their behavior is interpreted?

c. Neuman (2006) raises two other ethical concerns for participant-observation studies. These are involvement with deviants and problems with "the powerful."

Let's examine these ethical issues one at a time, starting with informed consent. Generally, an **informed consent** form should include the following (APA, 2002; Lewis, 2003):

1. Purpose of the study

2. Everything the participant is required to do

3. Potential risks and benefits from participation

4. Any situation where participants might be identified or quoted

5. Voluntary participation

6. Any anticipated factors that might influence a person's decision to participate

7. Any possible consequences of leaving the study before its end

8. Any inducements for participation (such as payment)

9. How the data will be used

10. How to contact someone to find out the results of the study

11. Permission from parents for minors

The informed consent form should include a statement that data are **confidential** and the identity of the person is **anonymous.** Confidential data include data from all stages of the study, including data collection and storage. The informed consent form should outline any conditions in which anonymity or confidentiality might not be honored. For example, if a participant in an interview reveals something potentially damaging, such as a plan to harm another person, should the researcher keep this confidential? One solution is to outline any conditions in which the person will not remain anonymous or the data will not remain confidential in the informed consent form.

The participant should be informed in the consent form of all expectations for the study, including any **potential harm.** Participants should feel comfortable with all aspects of the study and understand that they may withdraw at any time. Lewis (2003) says that interview research requires particular consideration. For example, a person may seem comfortable during the interview but later have regrets about revealing sensitive and/or personal information. Participants should have the opportunity to withdraw anything in the interview that makes them uncomfortable. In addition, participants may reveal something that is potentially harmful to themselves in interviews. Lewis recommends that an interviewer respond to these comments by encouraging the participant to seek appropriate help. If no disclaimer is made in the informed consent form, this is all an interviewer can do. Disclaimers protect both the researcher and the participant.

Fieldwork is potentially dangerous to the researcher, so it is important to consider **potential harm** again. Lewis (2003) recommends that if the study takes place in a public place, the researcher should have clear directions to the site and a clear plan for quickly leaving if necessary. If the study takes place in a private place, such as an interview in an individual's home, others should know where the researcher is at all times and when he or she is expected to return. Researchers should plan a strategy in advance for possible angry feelings that might be displayed during an interview. The researcher should respond to anger with empathy and perhaps move on to another question but must also know when to end the interview. Neuman (2006) adds that the researcher should not dress and act too much as an outsider, should create a safety zone of comfortable companions when conducting field research, and should perhaps even find a protector if the field research is in a dangerous place.

Participant-observation studies present some special ethical concerns. First, it might not be possible to get the informed consent of everyone observed. Participants may be those who come in and out of a courtyard over the course of a day. In addition, since one goal of participant-observation is to view people in their natural setting, getting informed consent can interfere with the study. For example, when Rosenhan (1973) conducted his participant-observation study, he decided not to tell the hospitals, concerned that if they knew he was checking up on them, the staff would alter their normal behavior. Rosenhan's participant-observation study used **covert observation.** This is a contentious point. Some feel that conducting observation studies without the consent of participants is ethical as long as the researcher does not manipulate anything in the environment and participants cannot be identified in the report. Others feel that the deception is difficult to justify. Coolican (2004) points out that after participant-observers disclose and tell others about the study, many people cannot recall what they said, when they said it, and what they did during the project. Thus, some participants cannot withdraw their data even if they wish to do so. Researchers using participant-observation often conduct **overt observation.** In this case, the consent of participants is required. Ehrmin's (2002) study of women recovering from addictions used overt observation, and she had consent. Ehrmin also had to pay close attention to the anonymity and confidentiality rule, as some of her participants had broken the law. In contrast, Rosenhan (1973) used covert observation, and he did not get informed consent for the first part of his study. He had consent to conduct follow-up research but used deception, as he did not send any pseudopatients to the hospitals, even though he said he would.

Gillham (2008) writes that researchers must consider **who owns the observations.** For example, if the ownership is a partnership between the researcher and the observed group, then it is important to check out the quality of the observations and interpretations with some group members. Then participants have the right to challenge selections for recordings and the interpretations. Viewing the participants as partners in ownership strengthens the **credibility** and validity of the study.

One thing Ehrmin (2002) encountered was the ethical issue of observing and interviewing participants who had broken the law, what Neuman (2006) calls **"involvement with deviants"** (p. 413). Of the twelve women Ehrmin interviewed, eight used crack, one used cocaine, one used heroin, and one used combinations of alcohol and cocaine. In addition, these women may have had knowledge about crimes. Thus, the interviewees had broken the law and Ehrmin knew about it. Neuman writes that there are special considerations for researchers studying people who engage in illegal, immoral, or unethical activity. These researchers might know about illegal activity, might have information of interest to the police, and sometimes might engage in illegal activity in order to gain access to the study group. Neuman (2006) calls this having **"guilty knowledge"** (p. 413). The researcher has to balance gaining participant trust with keeping enough distance so that the researcher does not violate personal moral standards.

Last, Neuman (2006) discusses **"the powerful."** Many qualitative studies are done on those without power, such as Rosenthal's (1993) study of the homeless. Some qualitative studies investigate the opinions of workers with little power. Researchers sometimes encounter the "hierarchy of credibility." Such a hierarchy exists when people in powerful positions feel that they have the right to create the rules of society, such as with the homeless or in organizations. When giving a voice to groups that are not usually heard, researchers must be careful of accusations of bias from those with power. It is an ethical dilemma because the researcher wants to give specific groups a voice but must balance this intention with the knowledge that powerful persons who may have something to lose can block access to participants or even discredit the researcher.

4

Triangulation

Introduction to Triangulation

→ Validity.

Triangulation is a way to make sure that there is enough evidence to make valid claims. Triangulation shows the richness and complexity of behavior by studying theories from more than one viewpoint. Psychologists have greater certainty about their findings if similar findings emerge from research using other methods, different samples, or different data sources.

Just remember that the concept of triangulation was first considered in relation to studies using quantitative methods.

This chapter is devoted to triangulation for quantitative research, including experimentation. The concept of triangulation is important for evaluating quantitative research, which makes up much of what students study. *Chapter 5 includes a discussion of triangulation in qualitative research.* Some unique issues arise when applying triangulation to qualitative research.

Cohen, Manion, and Morrison (2000) define triangulation as "the use of two or more methods of data collection in the study of some aspect of human behavior" (p. 233). They identify six types of triangulation.

The first type is **method triangulation**. This means that a theory is investigated using a variety of experimental and nonexperimental methods. The multimethod approach stands in contrast to the single-method approaches of some historical theorists. Single-method verification is limited. The works of Freud, Skinner, and Piaget are examples. Some or even much of their work is outdated because of mistakes with single-method verification strategies (called being method bound). Freud incorrectly generalized his findings to all people from case studies of Victorian females with mental disorders. Skinner incorrectly made generalizations about complex human behavior from simple animal experiments. Piaget observed his three children and came up with a general theory of cognitive development. Modern psychology validates theory through a variety of research strategies, including experiments, ethnographies, and correlation studies. Research about the causes of aggression and mental/physical heath treatments are examples of topics with a lot of method triangulation. For some types of research questions, such as those asking for specific causes, psychologists believe that experiments must be done first and then the results validated through nonexperimental methods. For example, Albert Bandura (1973) writes that we cannot claim to know anything about the causes of aggression without first isolating potential causal variables in tightly controlled lab experiments. But the results of the experiments should be confirmed through other types of research, such as ethnographies studying aggression in the natural environment. Another example comes from researching the best mental and physical health treatments. Would it be ethical to give patients any treatment that has not been studied in a tightly controlled lab experiment to see if it is a valid cause of any changes that occur?

The second type is **time triangulation.** Sometimes research is gathered during one specific time period or certain topics are popular only for specific time periods. Time triangulation ensures that the time frame is not the reason for research results. Use of both **cross-sectional data** (data gathered at one time) and **longitudinal data** (data gathered over time) increases time triangulation. Examples of topics with high levels of time triangulation are aggression and language as a cognitive process.

The third type is **observer triangulation** (or investigator triangulation). Examples of topics with a high level of observer triangulation include narratives, special kinds of story that help children learn about their culture that are part of the research on language; the contributions of the MAOA gene to aggression; and the contribution of the serotonin transporter genes to depression. When research is **replicated** by an independent researcher, observer triangulation is increased.

The fourth type is **theory triangulation.** Theory triangulation is increased when two similar theories have support or when two or more theories are combined to create a more comprehensive theory. Lev Vygotsky's and Jerome Bruner's language theories are similar and are backed up by a large amount of research. The general aggression model (GAM) (Anderson & Bushman, 2002) combines social learning theory with other theories to create a more complex account of aggression.

The fifth type is **space triangulation.** If a theory is studied in only one culture, it lacks space triangulation. Culture is an important determinant of behavior. Look for cross-cultural verification of a theory. Cross-cultural psychology has made many concepts conceived and studied in the West relevant for everyone. Conformity and social identity theory are examples. Look to see if a concept has been studied cross culturally.

The sixth type is called **combined levels of triangulation**. The levels are individual, group, and the larger collective or the organizational level (called *society* in lay language). Sometimes research is incorrectly directed at only one level when the interpretation should span all levels. Social learning theory has a combined level of triangulation. For example, self-efficacy and education are studied on all three levels: individual student efficacy, teacher efficacy and its effects on the group, and the collective school level (Bandura, 1997).

Advantages of triangulation include the following:

1. Triangulation reduces experimenter bias.
2. Triangulation gives a broader and more complex causation model of behavior.
3. Triangulation reduces **method-bound theories.**
4. Triangulation reduces **culture-bound theories**, theories that are based on the observation of one culture. For example, some critics claim that the term *depression* is derived from observations of Western behavior and is not applicable to everyone.

Thinking Critically about Qualitative Research

Introduction to the Key Concepts

Students of modern psychology study a combination of quantitative and qualitative research. This chapter is devoted to some important key concepts in qualitative research: generalizing, participant expectations and researcher bias, credibility, and triangulation. These key concepts are in bold throughout the book as they are used frequently.

To What Extent Can Findings Be Generalized from Qualitative Studies?

Good examples of generalizing from qualitative studies are discussed in other sections of this book. One example is Ehrmin's (2002) observation study in Chapter 7. Chapter 8 also contains a discussion about generalizing from case studies.

Lewis and Ritchie (2003) divide generalizing from qualitative studies into three categories.

1. **Representational generalization**, generalizing outside the sample (related to external validity, specifically **population validity**)

2. **Inferential generalization**, generalizing outside the study conditions to other settings (related to external validity, specifically **ecological validity**)

3. **Theoretical generalization,** the extent to which the concepts used within a study explain a wider range of social behavior

Let's look at them one at a time.

The concept "representational" has a strict statistical meaning in quantitative research. Sampling in qualitative studies is not statistical. Rather, "representation is not a statistical match but one of inclusivity" (Lewis & Ritchie, 2003, p. 269). Rather than use the word *representative,* perhaps we should call it **symbolic representation.** High-quality qualitative study samples are selected in such a way that the sample includes a range of views from a larger population. For example, Becker, Burwell, Gilman, Herzog, and Hamburg (2002) selected a **purposive sample** from a larger group of girls who filled out the EAT-26 questionnaire (reviewed in Chapter 6). This sample was specifically selected to include a range of opinion and circumstance and was a much better choice than opportunity sampling would have yielded. Becker and colleagues' purposive sample was symbolic of the larger group of Fijian adolescent girls, although not statistically representative of the larger group.

But sometimes researchers warn that generalizing outside the sample is not advised. For example, Hargreaves and Tiggermann (2006) said that the sample in their study of male body image (reviewed in Chapter 6) was too narrowly defined for generalizing.

A researcher increases the inferential generalization of a study by providing **thick descriptions** (a term first coined by Clifford Geertz in 1979) of the study setting, the observations, and participant responses (Lewis & Ritchie, 2003). Thick descriptions help a reader consider the extent to which the conditions of data collection are similar to those in other settings. Ehrmin (2002) devoted a lot of space in her research report to describing details about the transitional house and the circumstances of participants in her observation/interview study of women recovering from addictions. The report is thick with descriptions that allow a reader to imagine how women living in transitional homes in similar contexts might have similar outcomes.

Lewis and Ritchie (2003) believe that qualitative studies have something valuable to contribute to theories about human behavior (increasing theoretical generalization) specifically *because* they investigate the rich contexts of human experience. For example, biological psychologists are learning more about how the brain behaves when an addict relapses. But studies such as Ehrmin's (2002) emphasize that we must understand the social context of a person with an addiction to account for all the variables involved in recovery. Just make sure that **data triangulation** is included in judging the extent to which a study has theoretical generalization. The results of any one study should be checked against the results of other studies on a similar topic.

In addition to Lewis and Ritchie's (2003) three categories of generalizing, it is important to also consider the **reliability** and **validity** of studies when generalizing findings from qualitative studies (reliability and validity in quantitative research are also discussed in Chapter 9).

Lewis and Ritchie (2003) observe that reliability and validity in qualitative studies involve two factors.

1. Are the same meanings assigned to experience in one context also assigned in other research investigating the same topic in another context? Rather than expecting strict replication, qualitative researchers consider the **trustworthiness** of a study. Can we trust that experiences are fairly similar from one context to another?

2. How does the researcher interpret data? Researcher interpretations are an internal validity concern. Internal validity is increased through **reflexivity,** whereby all procedures are clearly outlined with **thick descriptions** and a researcher's personal involvement is detailed. Reflexivity "enables readers imaginatively to replicate studies" (Lewis & Ritchie, 2003, p. 271), increasing the generalizibility of qualitative studies.

Let's use observation research to illustrate how to *increase* the reliability and validity of qualitative research.

Neuman (2006) writes that **reliability** means having both internal and external consistency. Internal consistency means that the interpretations make sense, given what is known about the sampled data. External consistency means verifying interpretations by checking and cross-checking with other sources and researchers. Reliability of observed data depends on a number of factors, such as the researcher's awareness of the subjectivity and context of the observations that may interfere with reliability. These must be acknowledged and considered in making interpretations. For example, data from group members are always influenced by context, so good researchers recognize that someone may say one thing in public and behave differently in private. Misinformation and even lies from participants must be considered. It is important to sample different angles of the research site to get a clear picture, such as a variety of locations, a variety of people, and a variety of contexts.

Neuman admits that it is almost impossible to replicate field observation research. However, validity can be increased with careful interpretation. First, ask to what extent the observed events are undisturbed by the presence of the researcher. Second, get some **member validation**—that is, ask key participants whether the observed data are accurate. If participants agree that the selected data represent their real-life experiences and agree with interpretations, validity is increased.

Finally, the **credibility** of qualitative studies is increased through **reflexivity**, anything done to increase the **generalizability** of studies, and **triangulation.**

Explain Effects of Participant Expectations and Researcher Bias in Qualitative Research

Participant expectations and researcher bias are also addressed in many other parts of this book. Chapter 6 contains a discussion of these concepts in the section about considerations before, during, and after interviews. Chapter 7 contains a discussion of these concepts in the section about setting up and carrying out observation research. Chapter 8 contains a discussion of these concepts in the section about evaluating case studies. **Participant expectations** and **researcher bias** are familiar terms from quantitative research. Both are also potential challenges for qualitative studies and require special consideration.

Because the purpose of qualitative research is to discover the richness and complexities of real-life situations, the researcher's role is more subjective. Greater subjectivity might increase researcher bias. For example, interviewers using a semistructured approach might have a general list of topics to ask about but are open to the direction taken by the participant. Interviewers frequently use their intuition to probe participants for more detailed information and context. Because of this more subjective role, researchers should include a detailed statement of **reflexivity**.

Participant expectations should be considered in the planning stages of any study. Although qualitative studies are meant to be more subjective, at what point do participant expectations interfere with gathering credible data? For example, researchers writing interview questions should consider the extent to which any question might trigger **demand characteristics.** Researchers must write questions that invite genuine responses without making participants feel that they must give a particular type of answer. Researcher bias can be reduced in observation studies with, for example, the use of **thick descriptions.** Thick descriptions are very detailed descriptions that aid the reader in understanding exactly what happened at the research site. Chapter 7 includes two examples. First, Ehrmin's (2002) study contains detailed descriptions of data collection. Alexander, Miller, and Hengst (2001) took special care to minimize researcher bias in their diary-observation study.

One way to minimize participant expectations in observation research is to conduct a covert observation study, such as Rosenhan's (1973). However, the use of covert observation comes with special ethical considerations (see Chapter 3).

Explain the Importance of Credibility in Qualitative Research

Credibility is increased a number of ways:

1. Using reflexivity
2. Doing things that increase the generalizibility of the study
3. Performing triangulation that is appropriate for qualitative research

In addition to these three, Willig (2001) outlines some things researchers can do to increase the quality of their studies.

1. Make sure that the categories generated in interpretation are a good fit with the data. The best way to show that the data are a good fit is to provide clear descriptions of the process (**thick descriptions**).
2. Make sure to clearly describe the life circumstances of the sample.
3. Make sure that interpretations are checked against those of others or stand up to data analysis using other methods.
4. Explore the extent to which the study results are transferable to other people and contexts.

Robert Yin (2009) adds one more thing. An analysis should identify all rival interpretations for the data and show how they are not plausible.

Credibility comes up frequently throughout this book. The example studies include some discussions of increasing credibility. For example, Alexander and colleagues (2001) increased the credibility of their study by ensuring the reliability between the parent observers and the researchers (reviewed in Chapter 7). Credibility is also addressed in Chapter 3; creating a partnership with participants can increase a study's credibility, especially if the observed sample also agrees with the interpretations. A last example is discussed in Chapter 7 in the section about setting up and carrying out observation research.

Explain the Effect of Triangulation on the Credibility/Trustworthiness of Qualitative Research

Triangulation is important for qualitative studies, but we must be careful not to apply the exact same standards for triangulation in quantitative research. This material on triangulation for qualitative studies is also relevant for considering the **credibility** and **generalizability** of qualitative research.

There is some disagreement about using triangulation in qualitative studies. Let's first look at some reasons why some researchers caution against a strict requirement that triangulation be used to validate qualitative research. Then we can try to figure out a defensible argument about how we might apply triangulation to qualitative studies.

Some qualitative researchers argue that triangulation is not a very useful concept (Ritchie, 2003). Two key points about the nature of knowledge drive this view:

1. There is no single reality, and it is pointless to combine viewpoints under the banner of triangulation.
2. Each individual research method has its own purpose. The knowledge gained through one research method is not similar to the knowledge gained through other methods. Researchers using qualitative methods are trying to understand unique meaning systems.

These are valid points. So is there any way to make the concept of triangulation useful for qualitative studies?

Perhaps the best way to make triangulation useful is to think of it as serving an entirely different purpose. *Some believe the real value of triangulation for qualitative research is not in creating more certainty, as it is for quantitative research, but in giving the results of qualitative research more depth, an extension of the results.* With this in mind, let's look at how triangulation is appropriately applied to extending the depth of qualitative research.

Jane Lewis and Jane Ritchie (2003) and Robert Yin (2009) write that the following types of triangulation increase one's confidence in data gathered with qualitative methods.

1. Method triangulation
2. Data triangulation, the collection of data from different sources
3. Multiple analyses in triangulation—different observers and interviewers compare data collection and interpretation
4. Theory triangulation
5. Member, or respondent, triangulation—researchers check with the participants to make sure that their interpretations are consistent with what participants meant in the original responses

Let's use case studies as an example of how triangulation for qualitative research is applied. Yin (2009) says that data triangulation increases the strength of case studies. In addition, the need to use multiple sources in case studies is much greater than it is in other kinds of research.

The nature of case studies is to paint a rich picture of behavior. Richness implies that researchers examine multiple data sources. For example, Yin says that documents, archival records, open-ended interviews, observations, interviews, and surveys can shed different light on the topic of case studies. If these sources converge, or have similar findings, then researchers have a high degree of triangulation for their interpretations, far more evidence than using data from just one source. The use of multiple sources increases the credibility of a case study and gives the researcher more confidence in generalizing.

But keep in mind that using multiple sources is a lot of work for the researcher. Studies using more than one source take more time to complete and are more expensive. In addition, case study researchers must be knowledgeable about a variety of research methods, so their training must be extensive.

Think about some examples where data triangulation is possible. One is writing a case study about relationships between senior management and the employees in an organization. Observation, surveys of all employees, individual interviews with key staff, and focus group interviews with key staff can all be used to gather data about the company. Organizational psychology makes frequent use of case studies.

Chapter 8 contains two case studies that illustrate the benefits of data triangulation. Ma (2008) used data from many families—a multiple-case design. Cohen, Tenenbaum, and English (2006) also used data from multiple cases; in addition, they used interviews, questionnaires, and observations to collect data.

Explain Reflexivity in Qualitative Research

Reflexivity means that researchers are aware that their own biases and feelings affect the construction of meanings throughout the research process and acknowledge that it is impossible to remain objective while conducting research (Nightingale & Cromby, 1999). Researchers know that they impact both data collection and analysis. Willig (2001) identifies two kinds of reflexivity, **personal reflexivity** and **epistemological reflexivity**. Personal reflexivity means that researchers reflect on the way their values, experiences, political beliefs, and social identities influence the study. Epistemological reflexivity means that researchers have considered their assumptions about the nature of the world and the nature of knowledge that relates to a study.

Quantitative research is low in reflexivity. Researchers conducting experiments, for example, want an objective role; studies are designed so that the researcher has little impact on participant behavior and data analysis.

In contrast, qualitative research is high in reflexivity. For example, Ehrmin (2002) includes a detailed reflexive statement in her observation study on women recovering from addictions. Ehrmin writes that "criteria for evaluation of qualitative research were used to assure trustworthiness of the data, including . . . confirmability, established through the use of a reflexive journal demonstrating underlying processes, philosophical orientation, and the decision-making process in determining codes, categories, and themes" (p. 783). Ehrmin's journal helps others to replicate her study as much as possible.

Material from other sections of this book is also relevant to this discussion. Reflexivity aids in generalizing from research (also in this chapter) and is part of distinguishing between qualitative and quantitative research (Chapter 1).

6

Interviews: Qualitative Approach

Introduction to Interview Methods

The purpose of an interview is to ask questions to get someone's point of view. Coolican (2004) identifies five different interviewing styles:

1. **Nondirective.** Nondirective interviews are conversational, and participants talk about anything they wish. The interviews in many therapy sessions are nondirective, where the goal is not so much to gather data for a study as to help participants understand themselves. Results from nondirective interviews are often case studies of therapy sessions.

2. **Informal interviews.** Informal interviews are also conversational in nature, but frequently the researcher wants to gather data for a study. Although there are no set questions or a set response scale, the researcher has a general topic to cover. If the participants get off topic, interviewers use prompts to get them back to the research topic.

3. **Semistructured interviews.** *The semistructured interview is popular with researchers who take a qualitative approach, where the goal is to identify important themes for future research.* Coolican (2004) writes that researchers conducting semistructured interviews have a specific topic to investigate but questions are not asked in the same way to all participants. The goal is to understand the person's way of making meaning in a particular context. This leaves the interviewer free to engage in a conversation with the participant, and the participant might automatically cover the topics the interviewer is investigating. The interviewer will go back and ask anything the participant did not answer spontaneously. Legard, Keegan, and Ward (2003) add that semistructured interviews are meant to be flexible, interactive, probing beyond the surface level (with the researcher asking follow-up

questions for this purpose), and generative (creating new knowledge). Semistructured interviews can be one-to-one interviews, where the interviewer talks with one person at a time, or focus groups, where a group of people with a particular expertise are interviewed together. Some semistructured interviews make use of narratives, a particular type of story that helps people make meaning of their culture. Narratives make up a lot of human conversation and make sense as a research technique. Narrative-style interviews encourage participants to tell their story when answering questions. Sometimes narrative interviews make use of vignettes. Sue Arthur and James Nazroo (2003) describe vignettes as "hypothetical examples" (p. 129) that give focus group studies consistency. The vignette represents a typical case that someone might come across. Focus group participants then narrate (tell their story) about the vignette. Vignettes are useful for making sure that everyone in the focus group is familiar with the examples for discussion.

4. Structured but open-ended interviews. Sometimes interviewers ask preset questions to standardize interview procedures. However, these interviews still allow participants to respond in any way they wish.

5. Structured interviews. Structured interviews collect data with a predetermined scale, such as a Likert Scale. Structured interviews have several advantages. They are more objectively verifiable. The researcher needs less training to administer them. Researcher bias from emotional involvement is less likely. A disadvantage of structured interviews is that they lack the richness of less structured interview formats. *Researchers who wish to quantify the results of interviews often use this style.* Email interviews and telephone interviews can use this format. Anyone who is collecting data through email or from an Internet source must consider special ethical issues in addition to those discussed in Chapter 3. For example, how do researchers know if they really have informed consent for online research (Azar, 2000)? Participants check agreement forms, but how do researchers know that participants understand the intent and requirements of the study?

Which type of interview should a researcher select? *It depends on the goals of research.* All have a valid place in psychological research.

Interviews are sometimes designed and evaluated with the purpose of quantification. For example, a researcher might want to correlate responses from interviews to individualism or collectivism, predicting that either individualism or collectivism is related to the way that someone responds.

In contrast, an interviewer might wish to identify themes coming from interviews, where the goal is to understand how participants make meaning in the context of their particular life circumstances. This goal is important for qualitative uses of interviews.

Next are three examples of qualitative interviews. Each study illustrates a different way to design interview studies.

Note to IB Students

These interview studies are also useful for the Paper 2 learning outcome for abnormal psychology about the etiology of mental disorders.

Interview Study 1: One-to-One Semistructured Interview Investigating Attitudes Toward Disordered Eating (Combined with a Quantitative Field Experiment)

Becker, Burwell, Gilman, Herzog, and Hamburg (2002) studied **disordered eating** in Fijian adolescent girls before and after the widespread availability of television. As is sometimes the case, Becker and colleagues used both quantitative and qualitative methods. The research question was whether viewing Western television contributes to eating disorders in non-Western cultures.

Becker and colleagues first ran a field experiment. Female teenagers at two secondary schools in Nadroga, Fiji, filled out questionnaires in 1995, when people had limited access to television, and then again in 1998, after several years of greater access to Western television.

The second part of the study, the qualitative interviews, is more important to our discussion of interviewing. After data collection in 1998, Becker and colleagues selected a **purposive sample** of girls from the group that had filled out the questionnaire (the EAT-26, reviewed in detail in Chapter 9). They collected narrative data from a subset of these girls representing a range of disordered eating attitudes, eating behaviors, and television viewing. Interview questions probed attitudes and behaviors about dieting and perceptions of weight and body image in relation to Fijian traditional culture. Some example questions were "How do you feel about your weight?" "Do you want to look different from the way your parents think you should look?" "Do you admire any characters on TV?"

Several **themes** emerged from the interview data:

1. The girls admired the television characters and wanted to be like them by changing their hairstyle and body shape.

2. Fully 83% felt that television had influenced the way they and their friends felt about their body shape.

3. Another 40% believed that they could enhance their career prospects if they lost weight, and 30% believed that TV characters were good role models for how to behave at work.

4. All the girls felt that television affected attitudes toward traditional culture and that now there was a growing intergenerational conflict surrounding food consumption. This conflict was especially noticed in girls who had altered their attitudes about food consumption to reflect a Western attitude, with 31% reporting that their parents wanted the girls to eat more food than they wanted to eat.

Interview Study 2: Semistructured Interview about Male Body Image Using Focus Groups

Duane Hargreaves and Marika Tiggermann (2006) investigated **male body image.** Both experiments and questionnaires have been used to investigate body image, but the results are mixed. Most samples use females, and the methodologies are not the most suitable for understanding a boy's unique perspective. **Focus groups** were selected over one-to-one interviews because it was thought that the boys would disclose more about their views in the comfort of a group.

The study had two aims. The first was to describe body image investment, defined as "the degree of cognitive and behavioral importance that people assign to their body and appearance" (p. 568), and body image evaluation, defined as someone's satisfaction or dissatisfaction with his body. The second was to explore factors that were unique to male body image, particularly the role of the media and whether or not it was acceptable for boys to talk to others about their body image.

Three focus groups were created from 28 boys, aged 14 to 16, from an Australian public school. The focus groups, formed around grade level, included ninth, tenth, and eleventh graders.

A semistructured interview was used because the researchers wanted the boys to discuss the subject with one another in an informal discussion. Interview questions included "Do guys your age care about what they look like?" "How do guys your age generally feel about the way they look?" "Do guys compare their looks to friends/media?" "Do boys ever talk to other people about these sorts of things?"

Five **themes** emerged from the interviews.

1. *Body image investment.* The boys did not generally worry about their appearance unless they were trying to impress girls, and when they did care, they were reluctant to admit it.

2. *Boys' appearance ideal.* The groups said that an ideal male body was buff (muscular and strong) and that the desire to be buff was motivated by a number of things, such as sport competition, impressing girls, and self-defense.

3. *Media and body image.* The groups said that the media were a source fashion far more than the source of an ideal to judge one's body against. The peer group was identified as a more important influence. But only a small number of boys said they would do anything to become more buff. Instead, they were more likely to change their hair or clothes to fit in with peers.

4. *Was it okay to talk about male body image?* Appearance and body image were not considered acceptable topics. This was partly because it was not judged as important and also because of the fear of appearing feminine.

5. *Body image evaluation.* While most of the boys felt all right about their appearance, there were some participants who expressed concern about their body image, but in specific ways, such as size of muscles. Some boys said that their bodies were still changing, and they thought their bodies were changing more to the ideal (very different from what girls report).

The authors recognized that the focus groups may have kept some boys from reporting some of their greatest concerns about body image, but they felt that the study was important because it identified new themes.

The study's small sample from an Australian public school included little ethnic diversity, so the authors warned readers to be careful about generalizing the results outside the sample.

Interview Study 3: Semistructured Narrative Interviews Investigating Lay Perceptions of Depression Using Focus Groups

Elialilia Okello and Seggane Musisi (2006) studied lay perceptions of psychotic depression in the Baganda of Uganda and how cultural practices shaped views about appropriate treatments. The authors wrote, "Culture is the lens or template used in constructing, defining, and interpreting reality" (p. 61). Depression is one of the most prevalent mental disorders in Uganda, so it is critical for health care providers to evaluate whether using a Western individual style of health care services is appropriate in Uganda.

Semistructured narrative interviews were used with both individuals and the focus groups.

Okello and Musisi used purposive sampling to select participants for the focus groups, based on age, gender, and ethnocultural background. The authors believed that age and gender might be important factors influencing perceptions, so the focus groups represented different ages and genders. In addition, one cultural group the Baganda, was used, to "avoid diluting the responses due to ethnic diversity" (p. 63). Participants were selected for individual interviews on the basis of their standing in the community as people who were "opinion leaders" (p. 63). Five groups for individual interviews were created: village elders, traditional healers, local leaders, faith healers, and community health workers (laypersons trained to deliver basic services).

A case vignette of psychotic depression (though not given a specific diagnostic label) was read to participants in both the focus groups and the individual interviews. Psychotic depression was selected for this study because depression is common in Uganda, it is often undiagnosed and left untreated, and people are most likely to seek treatment only for the most severe cases.

The vignette described a person with the following characteristics. He or she suffers from a lack of interest in pleasurable activities, is withdrawn, and does not clean or take care of himself or herself. The person claims that the ancestors are unhappy and that the ancestors call for the person to die, calling the person worthless and useless, and blaming the person for past sins. The person sometimes talks to himself or herself or stares. Sometimes the person sees dead ancestors or dreams of them.

All the responses were recorded and verbatim transcription was used. Here are some of the results.

1. After participants heard the vignette, the discussion started with "What do you call this condition" (p. 65)? Participants in the focus groups and individual interviews gave similar answers, with most saying the symptoms were related to eByekika (clan issues/problems) and Lubaale (ancestral gods). When the interviewers *probed* the response, participants said that the terms were interchangeable and that the symptoms should be treated according to cultural practices.

2. Questions about the cause of the disorder generated the most discussion about why someone had mental disorders, including where someone might get help. Five categories were created:

   a. Neglecting traditional values

   b. Breaking taboos

   c. Mixing foreign and traditional beliefs

   d. Abandoning traditional beliefs and religion

   e. "Lost blood," such as burying a family member outside traditional burial grounds, causing the haunting of the family member

3. Questions about seeking help generated some interesting discussion about treatment. First, medical and/or traditional healers were named as the best source for help with physical symptoms. But a complete cure was believed to come from persons with access to the supernatural realm. Traditional healers and diviners are the only people with access to the supernatural realm. Participants were firm that hospitalization had no role to play in treating this illness.

The authors concluded that the study had important implications for treating depression in the Bagandans, including appreciating the lay understanding of mental disorder and understanding the need for social support from the family/clan system in recovery. A Western individual style of delivering services would be greatly underutilized by this cultural group.

Evaluate Semistructured, Focus Group, and Narrative Interviews

Advantages of using semistructured interviews include the following (Coolican, 2004):

1. A natural conversation provides a rich account of a person's situation.

2. Questions can be adapted to probe the context and meaning according to the natural flow of the conversation.

3. Participants are more likely to give detailed responses if they are relaxed.

Disadvantages of using semistructured interviews include the following (Coolican, 2004):

1. The **reliability** of semistructured interviews can be poor. It is hard to compare data from one study with data from the next, as each one uses different questions and probes. In addition, interviews take place outside a controlled setting, so it is hard to replicate the situations. There is no one way that qualitative research should be conducted, so design differences make it challenging to compare studies.

2. Interviews usually use small samples that are often limited to one culture or one school because of the time it takes to conduct them.

3. It takes more training to conduct an unstructured interview.

Advantages of focus groups include the following (Neuman, 2006):

1. People are more likely to express their real opinions in a natural setting.

2. Participants hear others' responses and might be reminded of something important. The group setting can help participants clarify their own opinions.

3. People feel empowered, as if their opinions count.

4. I add to Neuman's list the fact that interactions among focus group members can give the study more richness and depth.

Disadvantages of focus groups include the following (Neuman, 2006):

1. An individual's attitudes may become more extreme after participation in a focus group; this result is called the **polarization effect.**

2. Usually only one topic can be discussed at a time in focus groups. In questionnaires or surveys, many topics can be addressed at once.

3. Individuals have less time to talk, so individual opinions are not necessarily developed.

4. The focus group moderator may unknowingly limit what the group discusses **(researcher bias).**

Advantages of narrative interviews include the following:

1. Narratives allow people to tell their story. Narratives make up a lot of human communication, and they are the *primary way people make meaning* of their culture. Storytelling is a rich form of interview data. Okello and Musisi (2006) saw more meaning expressed when participants were allowed to develop stories through vignettes.

2. Narratives provide a window into someone's life context.

There is one disadvantage of narrative interviews: narratives are very personal, and the individual stories from an entire group may present coding challenges to the researcher.

Discuss Considerations Involved Before, During, and After an Interview

Legard and colleagues (2003) and Coolican (2004) suggest that researchers consider the following questions before an interview.

1. What qualities and training are important for an interviewer? Interviewers should be good listeners, logical thinkers, curious, interested, respectful of others, and they should have good memories. The best interviewer has good rapport with participants and "displays a sense of tranquility—an inner stillness which communicates interest and attention and which is accompanied by a feeling of being comfortable with the interviewee and the situation" (Legard et al., 2003, p. 143). The more unstructured the interview, the more important thorough training becomes.

2. The interviewer should learn as much as he or she can about the language and culture of participants.

3. How should a researcher direct the interview?
   a. Stage 1 is the arrival, where the researcher must make sure the interviewee feels comfortable and in control of the setting.
   b. Stage 2 involves introducing the interview with clear statements about the purpose of the study and getting the consent of the participant to continue.
   c. Stage 3 is the beginning; it involves gathering information that provides context, such as relevant background information.
   d. Stage 4 is the working part of the interview, where the participant is led through the key topics identified for the study. Here the participant works at a deeper level, such as remembering things not considered for a long time.
   e. Stage 5 is the ending, where the discussion returns to the surface level.

   f. Stage 6 occurs after the interview. The tape recorder is turned off
     and the interview ends with thanks to participants for their help.
     Perhaps participants need reassurance that their participation is
     confidential. If a participant remembers something important after
     the formal recording is over, perhaps he or she will need to say it
     again into the tape recorder.

4. Ethical issues are considered. Participants give consent, are guaranteed confidentiality, and are allowed to change their opinion at any
   time or even to end their participation.

5. Good interview questions and probes are developed. For example, interviewers should ask clear questions, avoid double-barreled questions
   (where two things are asked at the same time), and avoid leading
   questions. There are many different probes appropriate for interviews.
   One example of a probe is amplifying a previous comment from a
   participant, such as "Can you tell me a little more about . . . ?"

6. The potential for demand characteristics (where cues from a researcher make the interviewee anticipate and respond to what he or
   she thinks the researcher wants) and researcher bias to influence the
   study are considered. For example, an interviewer's gender, personal
   qualities, or ethnicity might increase the chances of demand characteristics coming into play.

7. Details of scheduling interviews are considered. How long will the interview last? Where should it be held? Is the setting for the interview
   safe for the participant and the researcher? How will data be
   recorded? Should anyone else be allowed to attend?

During an interview, Legard and colleagues (2003) advise researchers to
consider the following points:

1. The interviewer must create and maintain good relationships with
   participants.

2. There are two things to consider about recording the interview. If the
   researcher stops taking notes, is this sending a message to the participant that his or comments are unimportant? If video-recording
   equipment is used, to what extent is it dominating the room?

3. The interviewer must continue to think about the staging process.

4. Throughout the interview, the researcher must be aware of the fine
   line between showing empathy and becoming overly involved with
   participants. For example, if a participant expresses a position or
   feeling that is different from that of the researcher, it is important
   that the researcher not express his or her views and feelings. An em-

pathetic position is best, which involves probing to find out more about the participant's position and feelings.

5. The researcher may need to manage sensitive issues in two areas. First, the topic may be sensitive. The researcher has consent to discuss the topic but may need to lessen a participant's embarrassment or unease with empathy, such as saying, "I know this is difficult, but could you tell me . . . ?" Second, a participant may show a strong emotional response, such as anxiety or anger. The researcher can ease anxiety by acknowledging that the topic is difficult and sharing some general information about how other people have felt about the topic. A researcher should not take it personally if a participant becomes upset or angry; instead, the researcher should defuse the situation by acknowledging the feelings and allowing exploration.

After an interview, Legard and colleagues (2003) advise researchers to consider the following points:

1. The researcher must ensure that the end of the interview goes smoothly. Participants should feel that their help is appreciated, should have information about finding out the results of the study, and should have information about how to withdraw data if desired.

2. Researchers must decide how to transcribe data and then code it into thematic categories. There are two choices, **verbatim transcription** (traditional transcription), where the exact words are transcribed and nothing else, and **postmodern transcription**. In verbatim transcription, researchers transcribe the exact spoken words of subjects. It is quicker than the postmodern approach. Verbatim transcription does not take into account subtle and often important nonverbal communications, such as voice tone, posture, and pauses. In postmodern transcription, researchers record words and pauses, along with the "um's." This gives richness to traditional transcription. The researcher must decide before the study which of the subtle nonverbal messages to record, such voice tone, posture, and pauses. The entire interview is transcribed, not just the surface words. There are some potential weaknesses to the postmodern approach. It is desirable to have high interrater reliability between the transcriptions of independent raters. Interviews must also be transcribed soon after data are collected so that researchers do not forget the subtleties observed in the interviews. The discussion under the next learning outcome provides details about analyzing interview data.

Explain How Researchers Use Inductive Content Analysis (Thematic Analysis) on Interview Transcripts

All three of the preceding examples of semistructured interviews used **inductive content analysis** to analyze data. Induction is a "bottom-up" approach whereby important **themes** emerge from data analysis of interview transcripts. Although there is no one accepted way to analyze data from qualitative studies, over time guidelines have become more precise (Neuman, 2006).

Qualitative data analysis has the following goals (Neuman, 2006). These goals are very different from data analysis in quantitative studies.

1. Qualitative data analysis is *less standardized* and *more inductive* than in quantitative data analysis.

2. Qualitative researchers think about *emerging patterns* as they gather data and might even probe interviewees about new ideas that emerge. In quantitative research, data analysis takes place only after all the data are gathered.

3. The goal of qualitative analysis is to *create good generalizations* about a person's or group's experience. These generalizations are considered plausible explanations, and researchers give supporting evidence to minimize alternative explanations.

4. Qualitative researchers analyze data by *organizing it into* **categories** *according to important* **themes** that emerge from thinking about the data. All the interpretations are grounded in the data rather than in a theory that might be guiding an experimenter.

5. While quantitative data is organized into numerical units for statistical analysis, qualitative researchers *organize raw data from transcripts into categories and themes that make the data manageable*. **Coding** is central to organizing raw data into coherent categories based on themes. Coding is hard work and is time-consuming. On the next page, you will find a four-stage process for coding. To sum up, the researcher wants to make meaning out of the transcripts and uses a coding system to create categories about important emerging themes.

One popular method for inductive content analysis is **interpretative phenomenological analysis** (IPA) (Willig, 2001). IPA first surfaced as a philosophical concept but became popular with psychologists because it gave them a way to understand a person's unique experience of the world. *IPA is a researcher's interpretation of someone's experiences of a phenomenon*.

Researchers using IPA make some assumptions about the nature of knowledge. IPA is concerned with a person's subjective reality. IPA assumes that individuals can have different subjective experiences about the same objective reality and that these subjective experiences are possible because all reality is filtered through each person's unique beliefs and expectations. The researcher's role is to understand the subjective experiences, and to do this, the researcher must become engaged with the participant's experience (meaning that the researcher is not objective).

IPA involves a series of four stages for how a researcher creates meaningful categories from the themes that emerge from semistructured interview transcripts.

1. In stage 1, researchers read and reread the transcripts. This is a time of reflection. The researcher takes time to comment and ask questions about the interview transcript. Notes at this stage are unfocused; their purpose is to document first impressions.

2. In stage 2, researchers identify and name specific **themes** that emerge from the transcript. Psychological terms are used to give general labels to the themes, such as "loss" or "self-efficacy."

3. In stage 3, researchers impose structure on the general themes from stage 2. Sometimes several general themes come together naturally into categories (clusters of themes). If this happens, the researcher comes up with a name for the category, such as "cultural expectations," "media influences," or "childhood experiences." Some of the categories might be grouped together, as, for example, "the early years."

4. In stage 4, researchers create a summary table of the theme categories along with supporting quotations with a notation on where the material is located in the transcript. A summary table for a study on attitudes about disordered eating might look like this.

Cluster 1: Cultural Expectation		
Traditional culture	"what we ate at the festival"	lines 6 and 7
Parental vs. child beliefs	"what parents thought appropriate to eat"	line 9
Television models	"the thin girls get more glamorous jobs"	lines 10–12

IPA is not just for interviews. For example, Ma (2008) used inductive content analysis in her case study on eating disorders. Ma's study is detailed in Chapter 8.

Observations: Quantitative and Qualitative Approaches

Introduction to Observation Research

Observation is used in both experimental and nonexperimental research, so it can be used quantitatively or qualitatively. Gillham (2008) identifies many styles of observation, including the following:

1. Structured observation
2. Semistructured observation
3. The use of observation techniques in experiments
4. Unstructured observation, such as ethnography
5. Self-observation, such as diaries

Quantitative Use of Observation

Researchers sometimes want to quantify the results of observation studies. For example, it is useful to know the frequency of children's aggressive behaviors in play, which can be correlated to gender or other variables. At other times, experimenters measure a dependent variable through observations. For example, Bandura's (1965, 1973) Bobo experiments measured aggression after exposure to different conditions with an observation checklist. But do not call Bandura's Bobo studies "observation studies." The Bobo studies are lab experiments. Data were just collected with observation checklists.

Structured observation grids are developed to quantify observations. Items on the grid cover all possible behaviors related to the research question. An example research question is "To what extent is the level of aggression in play different between males and females?" Aggression in play is then made operational, meaning made concrete and observable, as shown in the following grid.

Aggressive Play in Males and Females		
Aggressive play	Male	Female
Yells		
Punches		
Kicks		
Threatens with toy gun		

An actual grid is lengthier in order to record all behaviors related to aggression. Every instance of the observed behaviors gets a check on the grid.

Researchers decide ahead of time whether to use time, event, or point sampling (Coolican, 2004; Goodwin, 1998). Researchers using time recording do not try to keep a continuous record of everything. Instead, behavior is sampled at predefined times. Event sampling means recording a specific set of events and ignoring all others. Preserving the details of high school graduation events is an example. Point sampling means observing an individual's behavior before moving on to the next person in the sample.

It is hoped that interobserver reliability (or interrater reliability) is high—that more than one researcher sees the same things. Interrater reliability reduces researcher bias. Bandura's Bobo experiments used more than one observer, and there was high reliability between the raters. Reliability is calculated as a correlation coefficient, and coefficients closest to 1.0 are the strongest.

Qualitative Use of Observation Research

Three different qualitative studies are detailed next. Each illustrates a different way to conduct observations.

Note to IB Students

The first study is relevant for the Paper 2 health psychology option about prevention strategies and treatments for substance abuse and addictive behavior. The second is useful for the Paper 2 abnormal psychology option about examining the concepts of normality and abnormality. The third study is helpful for the Paper 1 learning outcome about evaluating two models or theories of one cognitive process.

Observation Study 1: Overt Participant-Observation about Addiction Recovery (Combined with Semistructured Interviews)

Joanne Ehrmin (2002) studied the recovery of substance-dependent African-American women through observation and semistructured interviews. The aims of the study were to explore the recovery care needs of the women living in an inner-city transitional home for substance abusers and help them successfully complete treatment.

Ehrmin believes that there are three aspects of these women's recovery that require research methods focused on context. First, it is well documented that substance-abusing women are likely to have experienced abuse and rape before they start using the substances. Second, many women say they use drugs and alcohol to numb the emotional pain of their experiences. Last, little research has explored other factors that contribute to these women's substance abuse, particularly the death of their mothers when the women were young and racism. Quantitative research would not help our understanding of these experiences.

In addition, different cultural groups have unique recovery needs. This view comes from the "culture care diversity and universality theory of nursing." This theory suggests that care is best provided within the context of the patient's beliefs and values. It challenges a Eurocentric view of care in favor of one that is more appropriate for African-American patients.

Ehrmin took on the role of participant-observer in her ethnography, meaning an observation study of cultural practices (in this study, the cultural context of African-American women). The study used overt observation, meaning that participants knew they were being observed.

Ehrmin spent three years studying a transitional home in a large U.S. midwestern city. She attended the Friday afternoon "house meeting" and then gradually lengthened her stay to include supper. Eventually she worked her way into participating in many of the woman's activities, such as attending AA meetings, cooking meals, having meals with the women and their children, and celebrating birthdays.

Ehrmin called her level of participation that of a "moderate participant observer," meaning that she kept a balance between participation as an insider and participation as an outsider. In addition to taking observation notes, Ehrmin kept a reflexive journal to document her own feelings and biases.

Ehrmin used an opportunity sample of 12 key and 18 general participants for the participant-observation portion of the study. The key participants were the most knowledgeable. The rest included staff and other women recovering from substance abuse who lived in the community but had not stayed at the transitional home.

Three to five interviews were then conducted with 11 of the 12 key participants. This part of the study used a purposive sample of the most knowledgeable women from the key participants. All interviews were audiotaped and used verbatim transcription.

Guaranteeing confidentiality was of particular importance because of the potential legal consequences from the substance use. Ehrmin assigned participants numbers and used the numbers in the coding phase of data analysis to prevent anyone from being identified.

Ehrmin's study has a high level of credibility. Here are three things that Ehrmin did to increase the credibility in her study.

1. Ehrmin increased the certainty of the findings by observing participants over a three-year period and documenting the important context issues throughout the study.

2. Ehrmin increased the ability to generalize findings with a purposive sample that met specific guidelines and also gathered rich detailed data (over 1,000 pages of transcripts just for the interviews).

3. Ehrmin kept a reflexive journal.

The results included two main themes and numerous subthemes, some of which are listed here.

1. One main theme was that the women needed to work through the emotional pain of their abuses and losses.

2. A second main theme was that working through emotional pain gave the women an understanding of the context for their use of drugs and alcohol.

3. One subtheme was the death of loved ones.

4. A second subtheme was racism.

5. A third subtheme was rejection.

Ehrmin concluded that working through emotional pain was a key factor for the recovery of African-American substance abusers because of their high rates of using drugs and alcohol to escape from difficult life situations. The women needed treatment that helped them experience pain rather than numb it. In addition, Ehrmin deteremined that these women faced "cultural pain" associated with racism and discrimination that should be part of understanding the context of their recovery.

Observation Study 2: Covert Participant-Observation Research about Mental Health Diagnosis

David Rosenhan (1973) conducted a **covert observation** to investigate problems in diagnosing and classifying mental disorders. Although this study is older and Rosenhan does not use the language of modern qualitative research, it is an excellent example of covert observation and very popular with students. Rosenhan's study is free on the Internet.

Rosenhan asked the question "Do the salient characteristics that lead to diagnosis reside in the patients themselves or in the environments and contexts in which observers find them" (p. 1)?

Eight people were recruited to attempt admission into 12 hospitals in five states on the East and West coasts. The pseudopatients were three psychologists, a pediatrician, a psychiatrist, a painter, and a housewife. Three were women and five were men. All adopted pseudonyms. Would the pseudopatients get admitted? How would they be treated? How long would it take to get released?

All pseudopatients called the hospitals and made appointments. Upon arrival, everyone gave the same symptom—that he or she heard voices that said "thud," "empty," and "hollow." Other than this fake symptom, pseudonyms, and false employment information, all other information was real, such as details about family relationships and a variety of typical life frustrations and successes. Everyone was admitted, and all but one person received the diagnosis of schizophrenia. The length of stays varied from 7 to 52 days, with an average of 19.

Once admitted, none of the pseudopatients showed any symptoms of mental disorder. So no one's insanity was detected because of abnormal behavior. In fact, many of the regular patients voiced suspicion that the pseudopatients were fakes.

The staff made regular notes about the pseudopatients, and an example of how they were viewed follows. One pseudopatient described his normal relationship with his parents to a staff doctor. He described a close relationship with his mother but a more remote relationship with his father. However, as a teenager, the man and his father became close. He was presently married and had a warm relationship with his wife, with only a few disagreements over the years. Rosenhan thinks there was nothing pathological about this description, but when the doctor wrote the case history of the pseudopatient, the tone suggested mental illness. For example, the doctor wrote that the man had "a long history of considerable ambivalence in close relationships, which began in early childhood. A warm relationship with his mother cools during his adolescence. A distant relationship with his father is described as becoming very intense" (p. 5).

Rosenhan also found that when real patients went "berserk," the staff treated it as a symptom of their illness, rather than inquiring into any situations that might have contributed to the outburst, such as mistreatment from staff. In addition, there were strict lines separating staff and patients. Staff left their glassed-off stations, which they referred to as "time out of the cage," only 11.3% of the time. The "time out of the cage" was rarely spent interacting with patients. Rather, it was spent fulfilling staff duties.

When pseudopatients addressed staff with typical questions, such as "Could you tell me when I will be eligible for grounds privileges?" they were answered with responses such as "Good morning, Dave, how are you?"

As you might imagine, Rosenhan's study was a serious challenge to the hospitals in two main ways (Hock, 2005). First, it did not appear that people with mental disorders could be distinguished from people without them; classification systems did not help medical practitioners tell who had a disorder and who did not. Second, Rosenhan pointed out that a diagnostic label had severe consequences for the person. The staff treated each patient as if the label represented the real person, ignoring any situational factor that might be relevant to interpreting behavior.

Rosenhan replicated his findings several times between 1973 and 1975. When staff at one hospital claimed that they could not have made such mistakes, Rosenhan said that he would run the study again, but this time a little differently. Rosenhan warned staff that he would send pseudopatients to them over a three-month period. The staff was asked to rate the likelihood that each admitted patient was a pseudopatient using a scale of 1–10. After three months and 193 patients admitted, 41 were judged as fakes. In reality, Rosenhan sent no pseudopatients!

This study is still ethically contentious. A critical ethical concern was the undisclosed researcher roles; hospital staff were deceived. Here are some questions to ask when evaluating the ethics of the study.

1. Did the benefits of the study outweigh the right of the hospital staff to give their informed consent for the study?
2. To what extent was it important to have the trust of those studied?
3. Did Rosenhan protect the confidentiality and anonymity of the staff and hospital properly?
4. Were proper safeguards in place to protect the pseudopatients from harm?

Observation Study 3: Use of Diary-Observation to Investigate Children's Experiences with Stories (Combined with Semistructured Interviews)

In this study about language, Alexander, Miller, and Hengst (2001) wanted to understand more about children's experiences with stories. Stories are an important source of information about cultural expectations. As a result, children seem to develop close "emotional attachments to stories and the cultural beliefs and practices which surround such attachments" (p. 1). There is already a large body of research on children's narratives (special stories that aid in understanding cultural practices). But it is just assumed that besides aiding in cultural understanding, the children have emotional attachments to these stories and that these emotional attachments aid children in managing day-to-day stressors and traumatic events. Alexander and colleagues sought more support for the assumption.

Stories are a shared experience between parent and child. The authors expanded previous research about the social significance of children's story attachments by including parent belief systems and practices related to their children and stories. Studying children and parental behavior together is based on Lev Vygotsky's theory that children learn what is expected of them from daily family routines where stories between parents and children make up most of the conversations.

Participants in the first part of the study, the interviews, were 32 families with preschool-age children. They were selected from a participant file at a midwestern U.S. university, perhaps based on who was willing to be in the study and probably an opportunity sample. Five mothers from the original 32 families participated in the second part of the study, the diary-observation phase. These mothers were selected because they had expressed interest in the study topic, had the time to record observations in their diaries, and had a good relationship with the researcher. These mothers were paid $100 per month for two months of participation. Three girls and two boys were observed by their mothers. These participants were Emily (age 3.7), Cheslia (2.7), Isabelle (3.2), Trevor (3.8), and Jeffrey (2.11). The names of the children were changed to ensure confidentiality.

Phase 1 of the study consisted of semistructured interviews with the parents and conducted in the home. Researchers audiorecorded the sessions and also took field notes. Researchers told the mothers that they were most interested in stories to which their children showed strong attachments and in which they had a strong interest. The mothers then selected the stories they felt were most important to discuss.

There were three sets of interview questions about these special stories.

1. *Family narrative practices.* Questions asked for information, for example, "How often do you read to the child, what do you read, and in what setting?"

2. *Basic information about the story attachments.* Questions asked included "What are the title and plot?" "How long was the child attached to the story and how did the child express the attachments (such as in his or her play)?"

3. *Mother's beliefs and practices.* Questions included "Why do you think your child is attached to a particular story?" "What were your reactions to your child's repetitive interest in a story?"

The five mothers participating in the diary-observation phase were trained as research assistants. Then they recorded observations of their child's emotional attachments to stories for two months. A diary-observation form was used by all the mothers. The form included the following items:

1. Basic information, such as the title and content of the story, as well as its form (book, video, etc.)

2. A checklist of what the child did in reaction to the story, such as telling/repeating the story to himself or herself or another person, asking questions about the story, listening to and looking intently at the book or video, and creating a new story using the original story characters

3. The feelings the child expressed

4. Behaviors suggesting that the child was tuned in to the story

The **reliability** of the observations was measured to increase the **credibility** of the study. Twice, a researcher and a mother independently made the same observations of the story engagement. The reliability coefficients were high, ranging from .80 to .95 (these are correlations, and the strongest correlations are closest to 1).

Coding of data from both the interviews and the diary-observations was done separately.

Verbatim transcription was used for the interviews. Some details from the interviews were tallied as frequencies, such as how often the parent read to the child. Next, the parts of the transcripts about story attachments were pulled out for more detailed analysis. Eleven **categories** emerged from children's expression of story attachments. They include requesting a story, expressing feelings, sleeping with the book, and pretending/acting out the story.

Important **themes** (the narrative interests of the children) emerged from analyzing the diary-observations. For example, one story reported by the mothers was the video *Land before Time*. Playing with toy dinosaurs was coded as part of the theme "dinosaurs." Another theme involved how the stories helped the children relax. One mother wrote that her daughter could personalize a story about a cat and a dog because they really had a cat and a dog. A last example is the theme of identifying with another's emotions. Several mothers said their children were attached to the story about **Bambi** and cried out every time they reached the part of the story when hunters killed Bambi's mother.

The authors concluded that their findings were similar to the findings of previous case studies on the topic, increasing the **method triangulation** for their themes. The American families had strong attachments to stories, and these stories were part of daily complex social practices the children were learning.

Alexander and colleagues feel that the greatest strength of their study was its **ecological validity**. In addition, several things increased the **trustworthiness** of the interviews and diary-observations. For example, the mothers were trained research assistants who elaborated at length about the story attachments and even admitted to some discrepancies in the data. Even though the mothers considered video watching to be less socially desirable than reading books, they talked equally about their children's use of both, lessening **researcher bias**.

The authors felt that one weakness of the study was that the diary-observations were so time-consuming that the practice limited the number of mothers who could participate in the study. In addition, the interviews gave researchers less detail about the children's behavior because they relied on the immediately accessible memories of the mothers.

Evaluate Participant, Nonparticipant, Naturalistic, Overt and, Covert Observations

Let's take these observations one at a time.

Taking the role of a participant-observer includes the following advantages:

1. Participant-observation studies have high **ecological validity**.
2. Participant-observation studies reduce problems associated with **participant expectancy**, especially if the observation is covert.
3. Covert participant-observation increases the **reliability** and **validity** of the observations; they are more like real life.

Taking the role of a participant-observer includes the following disadvantages:

1. **Ethics** is a concern in using **covert observations**.
2. Researchers cannot assume that they blend in with the observed group well enough to eliminate **participant expectancy**.

The role of a nonparticipant observer includes the following disadvantages:

It reduces ethical dilemmas, as **informed consent** can be frequently obtained.

The role of a nonparticipant observer includes the following advantages:

The researcher's presence may increase participant **expectancy effects** and cause participants to alter natural behavior, especially if the study uses **overt observation**.

Conducting naturalistic observations includes the following advantages:

1. **Ecological validity** is high as long as the researcher is pretty clear that his or her presence has not altered natural behavior.

2. Detailed accounts of behavior are possible, as in the diary-observations from the study by Alexander and colleagues (2001).

Conducting naturalistic observations includes the following disadvantages:

1. Ethical dilemmas increase if **covert observation** is used.
2. Data collection can be so time-consuming that only a small number of participants are involved.

Advantages of using covert observations include the following:

Participant expectancy is less of a problem.

Disadvantages of using covert observations include the following:

Ethical dilemmas occur with the **deception** of **covert observation**.

Advantages of using overt observations include the following:

1. **Overt observation** lessens ethical dilemmas.
2. It is the best choice for some types of observations. For example, Ehrmin (2002) needed her role as a researcher to be obvious. She spent a long time getting to know the women so they would feel comfortable during the interviews.

Disadvantages of using overt observations include the following:

Overt observation increases **participant expectancy.**

Discuss Considerations Involved in Setting Up and Carrying Out an Observation

Some basic decisions about the goals of the study and the role of the researcher must be decided first. Gillham (2008) writes that observational studies have several possible goals:

1. Exploratory goals
2. Descriptive goal
3. Evaluation goals

After a goal is selected, Neuman (2006) writes that observation research requires a large amount of preparation.

The following points must be considered in setting up an observation study.

1. Early preparation includes learning about the topic and defocusing. A thorough review of the literature on the topic for study and **defocusing**—emptying the mind of preconceived notions about the research topic—is essential for **credibility**. One way a researcher can defocus is to get a feel for the setting before deciding exactly what to observe. This helps reduce **researcher bias**. In addition, researchers need a lot of self-knowledge before starting the observations. For example, would any personal experience affect one's ability to be open to the experiences in the study? If the researcher had a family member or close friend with an addiction, might this bias him or her to another's experience?

2. The researcher must choose a research site and gain access to it. Three things are important for selecting the best site. First, the researcher wants the field site or group of people that gives the richest data. Second, if conducting ethnography, the researcher wants an unfamiliar site where the researcher has no prior expertise that might influence the **credibility** of the observations. Third, the site must be suitable. The site should be safe and must be physically accessible (e.g., there are no legal barriers to the site).

3. Decide on a researcher role. A researcher's role falls on a continuum between objective and very involved. A researcher might also be a **participant-observer** (blending in with the natural environment either covertly or overtly) or a **nonparticipant-observer** (observer-participant, conducting overt observations and not blending in with the natural environment). For example, Ehrmin (2002) adopted the role of a moderate participant-observer. The researcher must also decide what to disclose about his or her role and purpose. These are important **ethical** decisions.

4. Sometimes researchers need help gaining access to participants. **Gatekeepers,** people with the authority to give the researcher access to a site, can help. Ethnographers may also need **informants,** or people to translate when there are language barriers. Gatekeepers and informants may bias what is observed and interpreted.

5. Gaining access and planning for the actual study involve several steps. Neuman (2006) uses the term **access ladder** to explain the process. Gaining entry to the site is like being on the bottom rung of

the ladder and often involves gathering public data or paying a first visit. For example, at first, Ehrmin attended group meetings for short time periods. Only later did she gain access to the women's private lives. Climbing up to the top rung of the ladder involves establishing and maintaining good relationships with participants.

The following points must be considered in carrying out an observation (Neuman, 2006):

1. Build and maintain rapport with participants, keeping an "attitude of strangeness." Rapport building involves joining in with joyous occasions as well as sharing fears and anxieties. Unless the observation is covert, be aware that some participants will change their behavior during the study; this is called participant expectancy. The only way to completely eliminate participant expectancy is to use covert observation. However, sometimes participants get used to the researcher's presence and start behaving normally. But some group members might never be receptive. Neuman calls unwilling participants the freeze outs. Not everyone will be won over by the researcher, and it is ethically important to respect this possibility. In addition, researchers sometimes have to manage requests for favors from participants. Researchers must remember that familiarity can blind researchers to the things that are important for the study.

2. Make sure to collect quality data throughout the study. Observing is challenging. The best advice is to collect thick descriptions. Thick descriptions are extremely detailed accounts of the setting and context as well as what happened; they are obviously lengthy. A short encounter can take up pages in an observer's notebook. This way, the researcher is less likely to forget what is observed, thus reducing researcher bias when the observer recalls events. Otherwise, the constructivist nature of memory may interfere with the "true" observed events. Neuman also reminds observers to embrace serendipity. Researchers do not know what is going to happen and should not try to impose their preconceived notions.

3. Take rigorous notes. Credibility is increased if others can check and recheck a researcher's notes.

   a. Take jotted notes in the field. It is hard to take good notes in the field, but researchers create a shorthand to remind them of what happened.

   b. Write direct observation notes as soon after as possible (without having talked to anyone about them).

    c. Make **inference notes** when interpretations are made.

    d. Write **analytic memos,** which are decisions about how to proceed, such as "Make sure to follow up with Jane because she made an insightful comment."

    e. Make **maps** and/or **diagrams,** such as a drawing showing where everyone sat at a meeting, so that no one forgets important information.

    f. Keep a separate **reflexive journal** to make sure that personal biases and feelings are noted.

4. Focus on what is important for the study and sample appropriately. This means that initial observations will direct the rest of the study. In addition, Neuman recommends that observers use **theoretical sampling.**

Researchers have several duties after collecting observations:

1. Conduct interviews with key participants to discuss data interpretations. The study is more **ethical** if participants are allowed to comment on the **credibility** of the recorded data and interpretations.

2. Check and recheck interpretations with other researchers.

3. Debrief participants.

Discuss How Researchers Analyze Data Obtained in Observational Research

Inductive methods are the best choice for analyzing qualitative observation data. **Grounded theory** is one such method. Willig (2001) defines grounded theory as "the progressive identification and integration of categories of meaning from data" (p. 33). The goal of the grounded theory method is to create theory from identifying, refining, and integrating categories and themes.

Numerous strategies are important to grounded theory. Let's go through them one at a time.

1. **Thick descriptions.** Thick descriptions of observed data are crucial to grounded theory. Only detailed, thick descriptions lend themselves to quality analysis.

2. Creation of categories. As with interpretive phenomenological analysis (IPA, detailed in Chapter 6), grounded theory requires that categories be formed around common observations. At the beginning of data analysis, categories are usually at a low level of abstraction (descriptive). For example, one low-level category might be "emotions," including anger, jealousy, or anxiety. Emotions describe what is seen at the observation site. As data analysis continues, higher levels of abstraction emerge. These are analytic rather than descriptive. For example, Ehrmin (2002) selected the theme "working through emotional pain," which reflects a high leval of abstraction, to provide a way to interpret the emotions described at the lower level of abstraction.

3. Constant comparative method. The researcher moves back and forth between considering similarities and differences among all categories. This way, new categories and subcategories are not left out of the analysis. For example, Willig (2001) suggested that one category that might emerge from observations is "emotions." It is possible that subcategories will emerge. One example of such a subcategory is emotions that require an object (such as hate). Such a breakdown into subcategories ensures that all types of emotions are identified.

4. Negative case analysis. Researchers are always looking for cases that do not fit existing categories. New categories and interpretations might emerge from negative cases.

5. Theoretical saturation. Researchers code data into categories and use the constant comparative method until a point is reached when no new themes emerge.

Case Studies: Qualitative Approach

Introduction to Case Studies

Case studies examine an individual or group within its unique situation (context). Examples include an individual's or family's progress in therapy and relationships within organizations, such as a corporation or a school. The case study method is a good choice for research questions that ask "how" or "why" a phenomenon occurs (Yin, 2009). The goal is to get a complete picture of behavior, so many sources are tapped for data for case studies.

Yin (2009) recommends selecting the case study when you want to understand a real-life phenomenon in depth, but such understanding "encompasse[s] important *contextual conditions*—because they [are] highly pertinent to your phenomenon of study" (p. 18). Many variables are usually involved when someone starts investigating a case, so researchers use multiple sources of evidence, and the data triangulate as all the different sources come together. Case studies are popular with psychologists; they are a good way to understand individuals, groups, and organizations. Selecting the case study allows researchers to "retain the holistic and meaningful characteristics of real-life events—such as individual life cycles, small group behavior, organizational and managerial processes, neighborhood change, school performance, international relations, and the maturation of industries" (p. 4).

Willig (2001) outlines some specific characteristics of case studies that build on Yin's general definition.

1. Case studies are **idiographic:** they concentrate on unique traits of individuals or groups.
2. Case studies focus on context.
3. Case studies using multiple data sources have **data triangulation**. Multiple data sources converge for a greater understanding of a situation.
4. Case studies examine processes and take place over a period of time.

Cases are either **intrinsic** or **instrumental** (Willig, 2001). **Intrinsic case studies are unusual or interesting and are not easily generalized.** Cases of feral children who never hear human language are good examples of intrinsic cases. Feral cases are interesting and unusual, but they are difficult to generalize from because there are so few examples and so many confounding variables that could explain the brain damage to these children's language centers. **Instrumental case studies** examine how individual or group experiences fit with larger theory. For example, many case studies of therapy sessions, such as cognitive therapy, are instrumental because they symbolically represent people who use catastrophic and dysfunctional thinking. Instrumental cases are more easily generalized.

Many sources are appropriate to use in gathering case study data, including the following (Yin, 2009).

1. Documentation, such as letters, email, diaries, minutes of meetings, or mass media articles
2. Archival records, including U.S. census data, budget or personnel records, maps, and survey data
3. Interviews
4. Observations

Next, let's look at two examples of modern case studies.

Note to IB Students

The first case study is useful for the Paper 2 abnormal psychology option learning outcome about treatments of mental disorders. The second is useful for the Paper 2 sport psychology learning outcome about theories relating arousal and anxiety to performance.

Case Study 1: Case Study about Families Receiving Eating Disorder Treatment Using a Multiple Case Study Design

Joyce Ma (2008) studied parent–child conflicts between young people with eating disorders and their parents in Shenzhen, China. The goal was to analyze the meanings of the conflicts within the sociocultural context of living in Shenzhen. This case shows how important it is to understand the cultural context of a person.

Ma writes that drug treatment for eating disorders is not very effective, especially if it is the only treatment used. In addition, family therapy is more effective than individual therapy.

Ma created an eclectic and feminist-oriented family therapy treatment based on Salvadore Minuchin's structural family therapy. Structural family therapists make changes in the way a family manages stressors by rearranging the boundaries between family members. Sometimes dysfunctional families are too enmeshed (meaning emotionally entangled), and they focus too much on the behavioral problem of a patient instead of ways to resolve it. Ma's goal was to shift the family focus away from the child's destructive behavior and reframe conflicts that maintained the disordered eating behavior. Reframing means giving people a different perspective on a problem. Ma sought culturally relevant ways to resolve conflict to ensure that the therapy was relevant to participating families.

There are many studies investigating eating disorder treatments in China, but the recommended treatments are fairly ineffective. Some Chinese mental health practitioners think that hospitalization is the best solution. But Ma believed that parent–child conflict, particularly the mother–daughter relationship, was a main contributing factor. It is not helpful to blame the mother for causing her child's eating disorders. Rather, the mother–child interaction is reciprocal, meaning that it is a give-and-take process. It is a vicious cycle whereby the mother's behaviors intensify the child's behavior and the daughter's behavior intensifies the mother's reactions.

China has experienced rapid economic growth since the 1980s; one result is that people have more access to Western media, which comes from individualistic countries. As a consequence, intergenerational conflict is rising. The parents grew up in a highly collectivist and conforming China; young people, however, are more and more embracing Western standards of beauty (e.g., slimness). The highest rates of eating disorders in Chinese people are in Hong Kong, followed by Shenzhen (a region that has transformed rapidly from a rural setting to a metropolis with a market-based economy, while at the same time still retaining most features of traditional Chinese family culture, in which the family is dominated by the father's wishes), and then Hunan (which is still primarily rural). Shenzhen was a good place to conduct the study because it was still in transition.

Ma used a **multiple case studies design** for her study. She selected this design because it allowed her to draw data from many different sources. As a result of the data collection process, the study has **data triangulation**. The use of multiple cases also gives the study **analytical generalization** because replicatiing the findings of each individual case supports the same theory.

The sample consisted of 10 families from a larger group of 24 families that sought family treatment at a Shenzhen clinic. The families were of different ages, from different regions of China, and from different socioeconomic groups, although they were primarily from middle and upper socioeconomic strata. Ma used an opportunity sample made up of families that gave consent for videotaping and had attended at least three previous family therapy sessions.

All treatment sessions lasted about 90 minutes and were transcribed using verbatim transcription into Chinese and then into English.

Ma used inductive content analysis to identify categories of parent–child conflicts. The conflicts were originally coded into general groups, and then major categories representing important themes were extracted. Here is how the coding worked. First, Ma (2008) and her research team read through the transcripts and "marked off units that were related to the same thing (e.g., parent-child conflicts), and then divided them into topics (e.g., mother-child conflicts, father-child conflicts) and subtopics (mother-daughter conflicts in the lunch room, father-son conflicts in the lunch room)" (p. 805). By the end of data analysis, all the similarities and differences among parent–child interactions were analyzed, and any disagreements were open for discussion until the research team agreed on the final categories.

Three categories emerged:

1. Control issues and power struggles between parents and children.

2. Children's psychological development was growing more slowly than their physical development.

3. The desire of the children to pursue their own life goals within a rapidly developing economic society that was often in contrast to traditional Chinese cultural values.

These Chinese parents had problems with managing their children's disordered eating that were similar to the problems of Western parents. These similarities were seen particularly in the parent–child interactions in the lunchroom. For example, the therapist encouraged Mrs. M to try to get her daughter to eat a little food. Patient M responded with screams that she would follow her mother's directions only at home, not in the clinic. The mother then retreated and asked the therapist to hospitalize her daughter. Then the therapist encouraged Mr. M to try. The father was more patient and slowly was able to get patient M to eat a little food. It is typical for a child with an eating disorder to have a more antagonistic relationship with one parent than the other. Power struggles are typically more intense between mothers and daughters. To defuse and reframe the parent–child interaction, the therapist creates a small struggle between the parents and children in the lunchroom and then empathizes with the pain everyone feels. Then the therapist can help the patient understand the importance of getting assistance from both parents, who are also learning new ways to cope. Both parents and children end up viewing each other through a new lens. Parent blaming is avoided, and underlying issues, such as seeking independence, are reframed as developmental issues. The family is no longer focused on the eating behaviors.

Case Study 2: Case Study about Emotions and Sport Performance Using a Multiple Case Study Design

This case study is about sport psychology. Interviews and questionnaires were used to collect data.

Cohen, Tenenbaum, and English (2006) studied two golfers' experience with learning to self-regulate emotions. They asked two research questions.

1. How are different aspects of emotion (such as arousal level and pleasantness) related to performance?

2. Does participating in a psychological skills training (PST) program change emotions and improve performance?

The theory of the individualized zone of optimal functioning (IZOF) was the framework for the study. IZOF is a newer theory about the relationship between emotions and performance (Hanin, 2003). IZOF theory states that there is not one optimal level of arousal that all athletes need to perform. Instead, each athlete has a zone of optimal performance, with some performing best with higher levels of arousal and others performing best with lower levels of arousal. IZOF theory challenges theories suggesting that there is one level of emotional arousal that is necessary for all athletes to perform. Hanin developed the theory after observing elite Russian divers just before Olympic team selection. Some divers had high levels of arousal but still had high levels of performance. These divers were also self-confident and relaxed, interpreting high arousal as a sign that they were ready to compete. Other divers had low levels of arousal, but were also calm and relaxed.

According to IZOF theory, a number of factors interact to create optimal sport performance. There are five dimensions of performance-related emotional states, and they all combine differently in each individual: content, intensity, context, form, and time. As examples, intensity of emotion refers to the strength and depth of emotions and context refers to unique situations that affect emotions. The goal of training using IZOF theory is to create an optimal zone of performance for each individual.

Qualitative methods are the best choice for investigating IZOF because the theory is about an individual's unique experience.

Cohen and colleagues (2006) thought that a case study would help clarify the relationship between emotions and performance. This study is a detailed analysis of two individual's assessment and training. Since the case study uses more than one participant, it is called a multiple case design.

Cohen predicted that the IZOF model would be supported, that PST would help each golfer find her optimal level of emotional arousal, and that the performance of both golfers would improve.

Two 20-year-old females from the varsity golf team at a major Division I southeastern university in the United States were participants. They were selected from a larger group of eight golfers. These two women are a criterion sample, a type of purposive sample where the cases are important enough to allow for more generalizing outside the sample. It is assumed that the experiences of criterion samples represent the experiences of others.

Cohen took the role of participant-observer. The researcher took an active role with the golfers as a sport psychologist and volunteer assistant coach. This role increased the trust between participants and the researcher.

The study took place during four golf tournaments in the spring of 2002. Data collected during pretournament practice and the first two tournaments were used to create IZOF profiles. These profiles, along with interview data, helped researchers create an intervention program for each golfer. Three questionnaires were used throughout the study to help create the IZOF profiles and assist in creating interventions. One example is the Modified Affect Grid Scorecard, which asks such questions as "Please rate your mood as it is right now." Participants rated themselves along the continuums of pleasure–displeasure and arousal–sleepiness.

The procedures were as follows. Starting with pretournament practice, the golfers played hole 1 and then rated themselves according to the level of pleasantness, for example. They repeated the process as they played each hole.

At the midpoint of the season, each golfer's IZOF and psychological strategies profile was created from the collected data. Next, an intervention strategy was created so that each golfer could improve her performance. For example, player A (based on her high arousal zone) was instructed in ways to get "psyched up" for the tournament and at the same time remain calm so that she could channel her energy into productive play. Player B (based on her lower arousal zone) was instructed in ways to identify and control negative thoughts.

Both players improved a great deal, as shown by a change in tournament scores over time. The IZOF model appears helpful in maximizing performance. Player A performs best when emotional arousal is high and she has pleasant feelings about these emotions. Player B, on the other hand, performs best when emotional arousal is low and she does not report negative feelings about the low arousal.

Cohen and colleagues feel that the results support the IZOF model and advise trainers to help athletes create and work within an optimal performance zone.

Evaluate the Use of Case Studies in Research

Case study research includes the following strengths:

1. Multiple data sources offer different perspectives and increase data triangulation.
2. Case studies are sensitive to context and are one way to study how people make meaning out of their lives.
3. If the situation is unique, a case study may be the only way to research behavior.
4. Case studies help researchers come up with new theories. Much of what we know about psychology started with the observations of specific cases.
5. Case studies have good ecological validity because the data are gathered from real-life contexts.

At the same time, case study research includes the following weaknesses:

1. Poor population validity is the greatest weakness of case studies because data come from specific individuals or groups. But if the case is instrumental and data are gathered from multiple sources, the case has more generalizability.

2. Cases based on an individual's testimony are difficult to validate. A person's past memory is not always accurate, and people are likely to respond to the vividness effect. This means that subjects are more likely to recall items tied to highly emotional situations. This is why it is helpful to collect data from multiple sources.

3. Willig (2001) identifies several potential ethical problems. Confidentiality and anonymity are important concerns, particularly if the situation is unique enough that someone is easily identifiable.

4. While triangulation from multiple sources is an advantage of case studies, it can also be a weakness if the researcher emphasizes the multiple perspectives over context, which is one of the main reasons for conducting a case study (Willig, 2001).

5. Case study research is time-consuming.

6. Researcher bias is a potential problem. Consider all the possible sources of data for a case study. Could researcher selectivity become a problem?

7. Some sources of evidence may be difficult to obtain, such as certain kinds of documents.

Discuss the Extent to Which Findings Can Be Generalized from a Single Case Study

Generalizing refers to the extent to which the findings of a study apply to similar situations or people outside of the study. Case studies have the potential for generalization outside the study (Willig, 2001). However, we must distinguish between intrinsic and instrumental studies.

Although students are fascinated by feral children when studying language or attachment theories, there really are few feral children, too few to make good generalizations about general human behavior from them. The feral cases available are indeed fascinating and unique in their own right. Just watch the tendency to want to make general theoretical statements about human behavior from them. It is hard to evaluate or compare cases of feral children for many reasons. For example, any one feral child case could be confounded by diet, abuse, or exposure; any of these factors could contribute to brain damage to language centers, poor language skills, or insecure attachment.

On the other hand, instrumental cases have more potential for generalizing. The Ma (2008) and Cohen and colleagues (2006) case studies are good examples. Both used multiple cases, so there is more data triangulation. Ma also claims to have analytical generalization.

Willig (2001) writes that if enough cases show the same thing, then there is more chance for generalization. However, it cannot be a direct generalization to other cases outside those used in a multiple case design. The samples in case studies do not represent a larger target population the way they might in a survey. The generalization may be better thought of as a way to refine theory and give direction for future research.

Yin (2009) agrees; he feels that there is more chance for generalizing from cases if you think about the concept of generalization critically. It is common to question generalizing from a single case study. But think about it this way. What if we were to ask the same question about generalizing from a single experiment? In reality, no one should generalize from a single experiment. Good generalizations from experiments are made only from experiments that have been replicated numerous times. Yin believes that the same approach should be used for thinking about generalizing from case studies: "The short answer is that case studies, like experiments, are generalizable to theoretical propositions and not to populations or universes" (p. 15). The goal of cases is to expand theory, called analytical generalization.

Explain How a Case Study Could Be Used to Investigate a Problem in an Organization or Group

Use the case study from Ma (2008) in an investigation of a problem in a group (the family is an appropriate example).

Questionnaires: Quantitative Approach

Genetics and Cross-Cultural Research Are Two Places Where Students Encounter Questionnaires

Questionnaires are commonly used in research, but students do not always realize how often they encounter them because introductory texts seldom identify all the details about the methods used in studies; it would take up a lot of space.

Genetic research frequently uses questionnaires, including twin, adoption, and gene–environment correlation studies (where one's genotype is correlated with environmental factors). For example, questionnaires ask people about their alcohol use, aggressive behavior, language development, or depressive symptoms and correlate the responses to having a specific gene variation. Genetic research, however, is just one place to find questionnaires.

Cross-cultural research on the **dimensions of culture** also uses questionnaires. People are classified on dimension continuums, such as individualism and collectivism, on the basis of questionnaire responses. Cultural psychology research shows how psychological concepts apply to everyone, and questionnaires are used in many of these studies.

Note to IB Students

Genetics and the dimensions of culture are required topics for IB students and are just two of the many places you encounter questionnaires. The example studies in this chapter are relevant for Paper 1 learning outcomes about genetics, the dimensions of culture, and how the environment affects physiology, as well as the Paper 2 learning outcome about the etiology of mental disorder.

Introduction to Questionnaires

Questionnaires are part of so many lab experiments, field experiments, and correlation studies that it is important to understand what they are, how they are constructed, and how they help researchers collect and analyze data.

Questionnaires gather data about many human characteristics (Neuman, 2006):

1. One's behavior, such as whether you will comply with a request or whether you voted

2. Attitudes/beliefs/opinions, such as whether you eat diet foods or whether you think that bullying is a big problem on campus

3. Characteristics, such as age, marital status, educational level, and self-construal (for cross-cultural studies, *construal* means "understanding")

4. Expectations, such as what kind of education you expect your children will receive

I add to Neuman's list counting the frequency of a behavior, such as how many stressful events you have experienced in the last two years, and behaviors that classify a person as having a mental disorder.

Sometimes students confuse the terms *survey* and *questionnaire*. **Surveys** usually cover a wider range of topics than questionnaires and "test for current opinion or patterns of behavior" (Coolican, 2004, p. 169). A large-scale survey might investigate the **prevalence of mental illness** across a number of countries, such as a survey by the World Health Organization (2004) that is free on the Internet.

In contrast to surveys, questionnaires have a more limited focus. Questionnaires are used for many reasons:

1. Questionaires can categorize someone as an individualist or a collectivist (decided, for example, on the basis of one's independence or self-construal as independent), and the results are then correlated with a wide range of factors, such as self-efficacy, compliance with a request, or conformity.

2. Researchers studying the interaction between genetics and environmental factors (**gene–environment correlation**, one

molecular genetics research method) might use a questionnaire to gather data on the number of stressful life events someone goes through in a specific time frame. The data from the questionnaire are then correlated with the presence of a mental illness (also determined by responses to questionnaires) and a particular genotype.

3. Researchers conducting **twin studies** (another behavioral genetics research method) use questionnaires to assess the behaviors they wish to investigate, such as aggression or the incidence of mental illness.

4. Psychologists running field experiments use questionnaires to measure behavior change. For example, Becker, Burwell, Gilman, Herzog, and Hamburg (2002) used the EAT-26 (Eating Attitudes Test, Garner & Garfinkel, 1979) to see if disordered eating increased in Fijian adolescent girls after television became available.

5. A psychologist might investigate student opinions about a topic, such as school policies, the existence and severity of bullying on campus, or gender differences in choices of a college major.

6. Some questionnaires are **psychometric tests**, tests that are meant to be a somewhat permanent measure, such as intelligence or personality tests (Coolican, 2004). There even are standardized questionnaires to aid researchers conducting **cross-cultural research**, such as the Singelis Self-Construal Scale (Singelis, 1999). Psychometric tests take a long time to construct and require a lot of expertise because they must be **standardized**, meaning that they must have gone through the process of establishing **reliability** (the instrument is consistent with other measures of the same type) and **validity** (the instrument does what it claims to do, for example, actually measuring personality).

Examples of standardized questionnaires include the **Singelis Self-Construal Scale**, the **Diagnostic Interview Schedule**, now in its fifth revision, called DIS-IV (NIMH, 1997), and the **Eating Attitudes Test (EAT-26**, Garner & Garfinkel, 1979); all these questionnaires are discussed in detail in this chapter.

Next are three examples of how the psychometric questionnaires listed here are used in studies.

Questionnaire Study 1: Use of the EAT-26 Questionnaire in a Field Experiment about Attitudes Toward Disordered Eating

Anne Becker and colleagues (2002) used the EAT-26 as part of a study to see if disordered eating increased in Fijian adolescent girls after television became available to the public in Fiji. Before 1995, television access was limited in Fiji. When Becker and colleagues first tested participants in 1995, the girls had been exposed to Western television for less than one month. The 1998 sample had been exposed to Western television for three years.

In 1995 and then again in 1998, an opportunity sample of all ethnic Fijian girls from two secondary schools responded to the EAT-26 questionnaire.

The EAT-26 is a popular questionnaire to assess disordered eating. Google "EAT-26" to see numerous websites featuring the questionnaire; on many of these sites, you can read the entire questionnaire. The EAT-26 uses a **Likert Scale** with "always," "usually," "often," "sometimes," "rarely," and "never" as possible responses. Participants respond to statements such as "Am terrified about being overweight," "Avoid eating when I am hungry," and "Feel extremely guilty after eating."

The EAT-26 is standardized and is one of the most widely used inventories for assessing disordered eating. It has strengths as well as weaknesses. Although the questionnaire could show that it is a reliable instrument, it does not access a person's context. So there is a chance that someone is at high risk for an eating disorder, but in reality, poverty is a better explanation for some of the person's behaviors. However, no one questionnaire is enough for a mental disorder diagnosis; several tests would have to point to the same problem for a correct diagnosis.

Becker found that the 1995 sample had a 12.5% rate of disordered eating, while the 1998 sample had a 29.2% rate, a significant difference.

Questionnaire Study 2: Use of the Diagnostic Interview Schedule (DIS-IV) Questionnaire in a Correlation Study about Depression

Caspi and colleagues (2003) used gene–environment correlation methodology to examine the relationship among having the s/s allele (an allele is a variation of a gene), the s/l allele, or the l/l allele of 5-HTT (the serotonin transporter gene); having major **depression;** and the number of stressful life events. They found that people with the s/s allele who also had four or more stressful life events over five years had higher rates of depression. Participants with the s/l allele had moderate rates of depression. Participants with the l/l allele, even if they also had four or more stressful life events over five years, had the lowest rates. Caspi and colleagues believe that having the s/s allele increases one's reactivity to stress and having the l/l allele is a protective factor against depression. The sample was from a New Zealand database. Of interest to our discussion about questionnaires is Caspi's use of the **Diagnostic Interview Schedule** (DIS-IV, Washington University in St. Louis, n.d.). The DIS-IV is a commonly used questionnaire that tells us if someone has a major psychiatric disorder listed in the *Diagnostic and Statistical Manual of Mental Disorders* (DSM-IV). The DIS-IV is the fifth revision of the scale, and it is aligned with the current DSM-IV. The DIS-IV must be administered by a trained interviewer, though the interviewer does not have to be a health care professional. The results of the DIS-IV are reliable and valid even when the person administering it is not a health care clinician.

The DIS-IV turns DSM-IV criteria into questions to which the person answers yes or no. For example, the DSM-IV criterion for major depression includes the language "during the same 2 week period" and "markedly diminished interest or pleasure in all, or almost all, activities most of the day." The question on the DIS-IV that goes with it reads "have you ever had a period of at least two weeks when you lost interest in most things or got no pleasure from things which would usually have made you happy?" Another example of a question is "Was there any time in the last 12 months when you wanted to talk to a doctor or other health professional about feeling sad, empty, depressed or losing interest in most things?"

The DIS-IV is popular and is also used in large-scale survey studies. For example, the World Health Organization (2004) created a survey called the Composite International Diagnostic Interview (CIDI) that uses the DIS-IV questions. The CIDI has been used to collect **prevalence rates of mental illness** throughout the world.

The DIS-IV is a good choice for research for many reasons:

1. It is economical to administer.

2. It allows patients to give an entire life history of symptoms, including when the symptoms first occurred and whether a doctor was ever consulted.

3. It is reliable with the DSM-IV diagnoses. The DIS-IV has successfully been tested for **reliability** and **validity**.

4. Although it asks about sensitive topics, such as drug and alcohol use, less than 1% of people refuse to answer the questions.

5. It is easy for the layperson to understand, particularly because it includes **vignettes**, that is, stories about the disorders.

Many abnormal psychology studies about the prevalence, etiology (causes/origins), and treatment of mental illness use the DIS-IV, so it is useful to know something about the questionnaire. Other common questionnaires used to study depression are the **Hamilton Depression Scale** and the **Beck Depression Inventory.** Both these questionnaires are standardized and use a **Likert Scale.** The Hamilton scale is administered by a professional and the Beck questionnaire is a self-report. The DIS-IV, the Hamilton, and the Beck are frequently used in the same study. You can see sample questions from all three questionnaires on the Internet.

Questionnaire Study 3: Use of the Singelis Self-Construal Scale in a Correlation Study about How Culture Affects the Brain

Joan Chiao and colleagues (2009) write that researchers know that individualism and collectivism affect behavior, but they ask, "Do individualistic and collectivistic values also modulate neural activity?"

Twenty-four right-handed college students made up the sample. Half were native Japanese living in Japan and the others were Causasian Americans living in Chicago. All participants had normal vision or had vision corrected to normal with glasses.

The authors did not automatically assume that the students were individualistic or collectivistic solely based on their nationality or where they lived. To find out, they administered the **Singelis Self-Construal Scale.** The scale is free on the Internet. Perhaps your class might take this test; it is fun to see how we are classified.

The Singelis Self-Construal Scale (Singelis,1999) consists of 30 questions—12 assessing the independent self, 12 assessing the interdependent self, and 6 measuring internal reliability.

Questions about the independent self include the following examples:

1. I enjoy being unique and different from others in many respects.

2. I can talk openly with a person whom I meet for the first time, even if this person is much older than I am.

3. I am comfortable with being singled out for praise and rewards.

Questions about the interdependent self include the following examples:

1. Even when I strongly disagree with group members, I avoid an argument.

2. I respect people who are modest about themselves.

3. If my brother or sister fails, I feel responsible.

The Singelis Self-Construal Scale uses a **Likert Scale,** where 1 point is for "strongly disagree," 2 for "disagree," 3 for "somewhat disagree," 4 for "don't agree or disagree," 5 for "agree somewhat," 6 for "agree," and 7 for "strongly agree."

Each participant receives two scores, one for the level of independent self and one for the level of interdependent self.

The scale has been tested for **reliability** and **validity.** One finding is that the scale has moderate internal consistency (reliability), which means that answers to some items are moderately correlated to others. Generally, we like to see strong correlations for reliability, but Singelis (1999) says that a moderate internal consistency is appropriate for this type of scale because the items cover so many areas. Scales that assess a single trait would be expected to have higher internal consistency.

Chiao and colleagues (2009) used responses on the Singelis Self-Construal Scale to divide participants into two groups. They calculated an independent self and an interdependent self score for each participant. Those high on independent self were categorized as individualistic. Those high on interdependent self were categorized as collectivistic. Seven Japanese and three Caucasian participants made up the individualist group; five Japanese and nine Caucasian participants made up the collectivist group.

All participants viewed 72 black-and-white photographs with 24 general self-descriptions, 24 contextual descriptions, and 24 self-descriptions written in either italics or nonitalics while an **fMRI** took images of their brains. All descriptions were written in English and Japanese. A bilingual translator ensured that the meanings were the same. For example, one general self-description was "In general I am assertive." One contextual self-description was "When talking to my mother, I am casual." One self-description in italics was "*I am truthful.*"

While in the fMRI scanner, participants responded to each photograph's descriptor on a 1–7 Likert Scale, with 1 meaning "strongly disagree" and 7 meaning "strongly agree." The photographs with italic descriptors were used as control photographs. One example of a control question was "Is this sentence written in italics?"

The results showed "that self-processing within MPFC [**medial prefrontal cortex**] varies as a function of SCS [Self-Construal Scale]" (p. 6). Individualistic values were correlated with greater MPFC activity for the self-description statements, and collectivistic values were correlated with greater MPFC activity for the contextual self-description statements.

The authors conclude that enhanced activity in the MPFC is a reflection of general or contextual representations in the brain, and they believe that differences in self-representation are related to cultural practices. This study is part of a growing body of **cultural neuroscience** research showing that cultural experiences affect neural circuitry.

Should Questionnaires Use Open-Ended or Closed-Ended Response Scales?

Should someone constructing a questionnaire use open-ended response scales, where participants write whatever they wish, or closed-ended response scales, which use forced-choice responses? Since the goal of studies using questionnaires is to quantify responses, most have closed-ended response scales, such as a **checklist scale**, a **Likert Scale**, a **semantic differential scale**, or a **yes/no response scale** (examples and a detailed discussion of these scales are provided in Chapter 10).

Closed-ended responses scales include the following advantages (Neuman, 2006):

1. Participants can fill out the questionnaire more easily and quickly.
2. It is easier to compare answers among participants.
3. Participants are more likely to answer questions about sensitive topics.
4. Replicating a study is easier.

Closed-response scales include the following disadvantages (Neuman, 2006):

1. The response scales suggest answers to the questions that participants might not have come up with on their own.
2. Participants who know nothing about the topic can respond anyway.
3. Closed-ended response scales limit the choice for participants. Participants might not find the answer they want to give.
4. Participants often give simple answers to complex questions.

Despite these disadvantages, which are valid criticisms of questionnaires, the strengths of using closed-ended responses dominate and aid in quantifying responses. **Triangulation** ensures that the results of questionnaires are not taken alone as "truths" about human behavior.

Coolican (2004) warns that participants filling out questionnaires are prone to the **social desirability** problem, meaning that they feel they should give the researcher what he or she wants. **Lie scales** are sometimes built into questionnaires to lessen the social desirability problem. Lie scales are questions unrelated to the studies that are placed among the real ones, questions no one would really mark as "agree" or "disagree." One type of lie scale uses always/never questions. Another strategy is to reword questions; the answers should be consistent throughout the questionnaire. Questionnaires from participants with high lie scale responses can be excluded from data analysis.

Sampling for Quantitative Studies Using Questionnaires

Which **sampling** techniques are best for questionnaire studies? Questionnaires are frequently given to **opportunity samples,** such as a classroom of students at a high school or students taking an introductory psychology course at a university. Sometimes questionnaires are used in studies with **representative samples.** For example, Caspi and colleagues (2003) wrote that they used a sample from the Dunedin Multidisciplinary Health and Development Study, a "representative birth cohort [a group with statistical similarities] of 1037 children that has been assessed at ages 3, 5, 7, 9, 11, 13, 15, 18, and 21 and was virtually intact at the age of 26 years" (p. 387). The Dunedin sample is representative of the entire population in New Zealand.

Purposive sampling is not as useful for questionnaire research. Questionnaires are easy to administer to large groups at one time. Purposive sampling is more appropriate for methods such as interviewing, where specific experts are desired as participants and where fewer people are studied in greater detail.

Standardizing Questionnaires

Questionnaires are frequently **standardized,** or tested for **reliability** and **validity.** The danger of using nonstandardized tests is that they rely on the expertise of the person administering the test. The Rorschach inkblot test, a psychodynamic personality test, is one example. Some nonstandardized tests, including the Rorschach test, are controversial. The DIS-IV and the EAT-26 are standardized. Check to see if questionnaires used in studies you read are standardized. Correlations are figured to tell the researcher the extent to which questionnaires are reliable and valid. Strong correlations are best.

Reliability means that the questionnaire has been tested for the consistency of items, both internally (among questions) and externally (similar results are obtained with other tests of the same thing or over time with the same questionnaire) (Coolican, 2004). One way to test for internal reliability is **split-half reliability,** where half of the test items are compared with the other half. One way to test external reliability is through **test–retest reliability,** where scores from the same group at different times are compared.

Questionnaires have validity if they measure what they claim to measure. **Predictive validity** is one example. Predictive validity measures the extent to which the scores on an instrument predict future success on a variable.

Evaluating Data from Questionnaires

Here are four ways to analyze questionnaire data.

First, questionnaires are sometimes used to measure dependent variables in experiments. Frequently one critical question on one questionnaire is compared to a critical question on another questionnaire. The Loftus (1975) eyewitness testimony experiments used this format.

A second way is to count frequencies of responses.

A third way is to use measures of central tendency (mean, median, and mode) and measures of dispersion (range, interquartile range, semi-interquartile range, mean deviation, and standard deviation and variance).

A fourth way is to calculate correlations. The total score or even one item can be correlated to another variable. Correlations show the relationship between two variables but never a cause-and-effect relationship.

This is a good place for a discussion about interpreting the correlation statistic.

Interpreting Correlations

Correlation is not a specific research method. Correlations are statistics used to analyze data, frequently from questionnaires. Sometimes books use the term *correlation study,* but the data are always gathered another way, such as with a questionnaire.

Correlation research examines the extent to which two variables occur together and how they occur together. Correlation studies show a **positive correlation**, a **negative correlation**, or **no pattern of correlation.** *A correlation really refers to the straightness of a line on a graph, so try not to give a correlation more meaning than it really has.*

Let's use examples about television viewing and aggression to see how to interpret correlations.

Many studies show a positive relationship (correlation) between the amount of violent television viewed and levels of aggressive behavior. This means that viewing violent television and aggressive behavior positively **co-vary**—as one variable increases, so does the other. *It does not mean that one variable caused the other to do anything.* Correlation studies are uncontrolled. It is not known whether television violence caused aggressive behavior, whether violent people watch violent television, or whether other unaccounted-for variables, such as genetics, parenting, or peers, contribute to aggression. For example, as the number of hours spent viewing television increases, so does the amount of aggressive behavior (perhaps measured by the number of aggressive acts children perform on the playground).

A negative correlation means that as one variable goes up, the other goes down. An example is the relationship between viewing violent television and creativity scores. As children's viewing of violent TV increases, creativity test scores decrease.

No pattern of correlation means no relationship exists between the variables.

There are two ways to analyze correlations.

One is a **scatterplot.** Researchers plot points on a graph (the point on a graph represents the two scores for a participant) and look for patterns. In the example of a positive correlation, a child may watch 8 hours of television each day and show 15 incidences of aggression on the playground. So a point on the graph is made where 8 and 15 meet. In the example of a negative correlation, a person may watch 7 hours of television each day and also have a creativity score of 20. So a point on the graph is made where 7 and 20 meet. Points are placed for the scores of each participant until everyone's scores are plotted. The straighter the line, the stronger the correlation.

Here is what a scatterplot for positive correlation looks like:

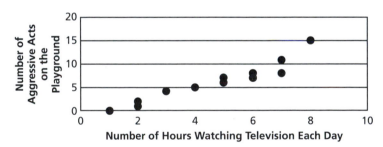

Here is what a scatterplot for a negative correlation looks like:

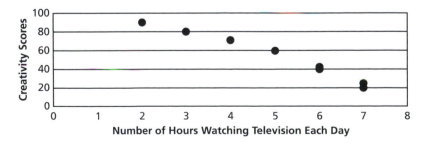

No pattern of correlation means that no line (pattern) forms when the points are plotted on the graph.

Another way to analyze data with correlation is to use a formula to get a correlation coefficient. *This is how most published studies report correlations* (even though the scores can be placed on a scatterplot). **Correlation coefficients** range from −1.0 to 1.0. The coefficients are not percentages, but they are interpreted as **weak, moderate,** or **strong.** Weak coefficients are from .01 to about .40, moderate coefficients are from .40 to about .80, and strong coefficients are from about .80 to 1.0. A coefficient of 1 is a perfect correlation. Positive correlations are expressed as +.70 and negative correlations are expressed as −.70. The interpretation is based on the absolute value of the coefficient.

Think of it this way: Correlations can be strong and useful to psychologists, but they cannot tell you anything about causation.

Square the coefficient to obtain the percentage of characteristics the two variables have in common. A correlation of .70 has only 49% of its variation accounted for, leaving much to chance.

John Brooks (personal communication, May 2007) warns that there is a tendency to overinterpret the meaning of correlations. For a correlation to have meaning it should be strong. I see the term *significant correlation* used frequently and have wondered what it meant. Brooks clarified that the word *significance* has a particular meaning in experiments, which is the probability that the independent variable caused the change in the dependent variable. The term *significance* is used rather loosely outside experiments, so check the strength of the correlation rather than checking for the word *significant.* The term *significance* in correlation studies is used differently than it is in experiments. For example, when experimental data are analyzed with a *t* test, they are tested directly against a level of significance, something that is not available in correlation studies. There is far more error in correlation studies, which is easily seen after squaring the correlation coefficient.

It sounds as if correlation studies have many limitations. Is there any way to increase the validity of correlation studies?

Keith Stanovich (2007) says yes. It is possible to use statistical methods to remove the effect of unmeasured variables that might influence the outcome. Three strategies are **multiple regression, partial regression,** and **path analysis.** These strategies are best explained through an example described by Stanovich. Craig Anderson and Kathryn Anderson (1996) used partial correlation to investigate the extent to which hot temperatures were related to violence rates, which are higher in southern U.S. states than in northern U.S. states. Anderson and Anderson call it the "heat hypothesis." They found a correlation between heat and violence, but their study had more credibility because they used the partial correlation strategy to remove some variables that might also influence violence, such as unemployment, education level, population density, and age. It is a complex statistical strategy, but it is important to know that researchers can increase the validity of their correlation studies. The other way to increase the validity of findings is to have **method triangulation** between the results of studies using correlation and studies using other research methods.

What are some advantages of running correlation studies?

1. Correlation studies are inexpensive and it is easy to gather the data.

2. Correlation research confirms other methods of research and is part of the **triangulation** process. It provides observer and time triangulation on topics where experiments are difficult. There are approximately 3000 or even more correlation studies showing a relationship between viewing violent television programming and violent behavior.

3. Correlation studies point to future experimental hypotheses.

4. They are used in research where it is not ethical to manipulate a behavior, such as self-efficacy or aggression.

5. Correlation is the only method available in some instances. Much psychobiological research is correlation. Genetic research uses the correlation statistic. The correlations generated on the role of genes in influencing behavior are best interpreted as increasing one's risk.

6. Correlation is a good way to relate questionnaire data to another variable.

Advantages and Disadvantages of Using Questionnaires

Questionnaires (and surveys) include the following advantages:

1. The structured format reduces **instrumentation errors**, defined in Chapter 10.

2. **Experimenter bias** is minimized with written questions.

3. Questionnaires allow subjects to remain anonymous and may help subjects speak truthfully when sensitive issues are examined.

4. They are an effective and cost-conscious way of collecting data from a large population.

Questionnaires (and surveys) also have disadvantages:

1. There is a potential **social desirability** problem. Participants sometimes feel the need to manage their impressions.
2. Poorly constructed questionnaires contain instrumentation errors.
3. **Ethics** is a concern. Many decisions about people's lives are influenced by survey results. If the survey is flawed, there is potential harm to people. It is important that all surveys be justified and well constructed.
4. Data are affected by a subject's memory and experience with the topic.
5. Surveys and questionnaires only measure opinions, preferences, or perceived knowledge.

10

Designing an Experiment

Some Context for Experimentation

The purpose of this chapter is to show you how to design a simple experiment that manipulates *one* independent variable and measures *one* dependent variable. Experimentation is the only research method that answers research questions about the *causes* of behavior.

Suppose a researcher is interested in investigating gender differences in math performance. Learning style is probably part of the explanation. Might specific learning conditions be one cause of female math performance? Since experimental design concepts are abstract for beginners, a sample experiment in this chapter investigates whether different learning conditions cause females to perform better in math. The design decisions are explained at each step.

Characteristics of Experiments

Let's first take a moment to define experimentation. All classic lab experiments share the following characteristics (McMillan & Schumacher, 1984):

1. Experiments compare at least two groups or two conditions. Either style works for an experiment about girls and math. For two groups, a class of girls is divided in half and tested with two different learning conditions. Then their math scores are compared. For two conditions, the same group of girls completes both learning methods.

2. At least one **independent variable** (IV) is manipulated. The independent variable is defined as what the researcher changes (or makes different) between the two groups or conditions. The IV must be something that can be manipulated, such as learning alone or learning in groups. Human features such as gender or age cannot be used as independent variables in classic controlled lab experiments. Gender and age cannot really be manipulated, even if they are the differences between groups. If you do not manipulate an independent variable, the study is a **quasi-experiment.** In a quasi-experiment, one does not know what causes the change in the dependent variable. Participants are not randomly assigned to conditions in quasi-experiments. Rather, quasi-experiments just test the boys versus the girls, for example. Many published experiments are quasi-designs, and they are quite valuable. For the high school student who is a beginner, it is important to know what a classic lab experiment is first. This way they know what you are adapting.

3. At least one **dependent variable** (DV) is measured. The DV is what the researcher wants to find out, such as the number of math problems solved correctly after training.

4. Experiments use **inferential statistics.** Inferential statistics show whether a **significant difference** between the groups or conditions exists. All raw data in experiments are collected in numbers (quantitative). Sometimes it appears that there is a difference between the raw scores or the means of the groups or conditions, but it is not known whether these differences are *significant* until an inferential statistical test is applied. A significant difference means that within a stated probability, such as 5%, it was the IV rather than chance that caused the change in the DV. If a significant difference exists between the learning styles, researchers know it is probably (with 5% chance of error) learning style that is causing the number of math problems solved correctly, not something else, such as teacher attitude.

5. Experiments are set up for maximum **control.** The IV is isolated from all extraneous variables that may influence the change. In the example experiment developed in this chapter, it must be the learning conditions that influence the ability to complete math problems, not another feature of the group, such as efficacy level or the number of math courses taken by the girls. *Control is the greatest strength of experiments.* But because control is high, experiments by their nature are artificial. Be careful about criticizing experiments for being artificial.

They are supposed to be artificial. Because there are so many internal controls (high internal validity), an individual experiment has low ecological validity and typically does not generalize well. Triangulation ensures that the results of experiments have meaning outside the conditions the study (ecological validity) and the controlled samples (population validity).

Conducting Experimental Research

The rest of this book is about conducting a classic lab experiment where one independent variable is manipulated and one dependent variable is measured. The sample experiment investigates the best way for girls to learn mathematics. This idea comes from reviewing literature on the general topic of gender differences in cognitive abilities. How do I get from studying general theory to a well-defined hypothesis?

Note to IB Students

HL students are required to design a classic lab experiment and analyze the data with both descriptive and inferential statistics. The material in this chapter explains in detail how to do this.

SL students are required to replicate a simple experiment, though the SL course does not require students to go through all the steps of an actual experiment. SL students do not create a hypothesis or apply an inferential test.

This chapter is useful to both HL and SL students. Both HL and SL students should understand how experiments are constructed and how the data are analyzed in order to evaluate research studied for Paper 1 and Paper 2 essays. In addition, it is easier for SL students to complete the internal assessment if they know what they are modifying.

The greatest challenges are in designing a well-controlled study, something both SL and HL students must do.

Quasi-experiments are not allowed for IB internal assessment projects. The researcher must have control over the IV. This means that the researcher controls the difference(s) between the two groups or conditions. Gender and age are naturally occurring, and if you place girls in one group and boys in the other, an IV has not been manipulated.

Introduction

The introduction of an experiment contains the aim of the study, a literature review, an experimental hypothesis, and a null hypothesis.

Note to IB Students

> The SL introduction contains the aim of the study and a detailed explanation of the replicated experiment.

Aim of the Study

The aim is expressed in one sentence explaining the purpose of the study. For the sample experiment, "The aim of the study is to investigate whether girls will perform better on the XYZ mathematics test after studying in groups or studying alone." A clear statement of the aim orients the reader to the experiment. The aim must be operationalized so that the independent and dependent variables are easily identified.

Literature Review

A literature review is an evaluative discussion of the existing published literature on the experiment's topic. The purpose of reviewing literature is to *justify a hypothesis*.

Note to IB Students

> The syllabus guide states that HL students may replicate an existing study or conduct a modification of an existing study. My own students partially replicate or modify an existing experiment. I tell students never to try to create

something totally new. Instead, I have everyone work in teams of four, and each team member is required to contribute something to the literature review. This means that each group has four sources on the topic, even if they will partially replicate one of the studies. Although there is no specific requirement for the number of sources to include in the HL introduction, this is how I structure it for my classes.

My SL students usually have one source. SL students describe the replicated study in detail instead of writing a literature review. This description includes the aim of the original study, the IV and DV, the participants, details about how the study was designed and conducted, results, and conclusions.

Review sources on your topic. Find something about the general theory on the topic and a few published studies. The review is an evaluative discussion rather than a list of prior research results. Focus the review on general evaluative statements followed by support from published studies.

Set the tone for the review in the opening paragraph. Introduce the topic with some general theory. Then make a statement about the existing literature. Is there a large amount of research on the topic? Are research results contradictory or do the studies come to similar conclusions? Do the existing studies use experimental or nonexperimental methods? Does conflicting theory need clarification? Do researchers suggest replicating certain aspects of published experiments? The opening paragraph drives what unfolds in the rest of the review.

The body of the review supports the general statements made in the opening paragraph. Write a paragraph for each area discussed in the body of the review, with transition statements between the paragraphs. These paragraphs cannot be just descriptions of studies. Rather, they should be evaluative, elaborating on the issues raised in the opening paragraph. If there are competing theories, say so. In your discussion, group together research studies that say similar things about a theory. Next make compare-and-contrast arguments. Assess the strengths and weaknesses of the reviewed studies. Current researchers offer critiques of their own research in the discussion section of studies. Suggestions offered in discussion sections of published research offer ideas for study modifications. Feel free to use these modifications.

The ending paragraph is a concise summary of the evaluations and a brief description of your experiment. The evaluations should show how you arrived at the idea for your experiment. For example, you might write that there is a need to clarify something, fix existing design mistakes, replicate a study, or look for new research areas.

The experimental hypothesis arises from the issues raised in the literature review. It is incorrect to think of a hypothesis before reviewing the literature.

Here is what I considered for the literature review for my sample experiment about girls and math performance: There are numerous theories competing for a prominent role on the topic of gender and cognitive abilities. Some theorists argue that hormones are the dominant causal factor. Others argue that causal factors related to culture, stereotyping, the school environment, gender schema development, self-efficacy, and parental behavior are dominant and exacerbate any inherited gender differences. A modern view is that all these factors contribute to mathematical ability. However, *even if all these factors work together, researchers can focus on only one aspect of the questions at a time.* The sample experiment in this book looks for an experimental problem simple enough for a student new to psychology to manage while at the same time advancing the existing literature. A well-focused hypothesis that examines one small aspect of the theory is required. Gender is inappropriate as an independent variable because we do not want a quasi-experiment to limit our ability to show cause and effect. It is better to focus on one aspect of the problem, such as the specific learning difficulties girls face. There is a debate over what factors are involved in the learning situation for girls, suggesting learning difficulties as a possible causal factor.

Research Hypothesis

Note to IB Students

SL students do not write a research hypothesis and null hypothesis. The aim of the study is sufficient to orient the reader to the IV and DV. SL students do not apply an inferential test, and it is less tempting to suggest that your prediction is correct without a hypothesis.

HL students need a research hypothesis and a null hypothesis.

The research hypothesis is a statement of the predicted outcome. It is either a **one-tailed hypothesis** or a **two-tailed hypothesis**, depending on whether the researcher can make a prediction or not. The independent and dependent variables are easily identified in the hypothesis.

A one-tailed hypothesis is a **directional hypothesis**: it makes a specific prediction that one group or condition will perform better than the other group or condition. According to some research on gender and math abilities, girls and boys learn differently. Boys may learn best working alone; girls may learn more effectively in groups. A one-tailed hypothesis for the sample experiment might be "Girls learning mathematics material in groups will perform better on the XYZ math test than girls learning mathematics material alone." The IV is learning alone or in a group. The DV is the performance on the XYZ math test.

A two-tailed hypothesis is a **nondirectional hypothesis:** it does not make a specific prediction about which group or condition will perform better. A two-tailed hypothesis states that there will be *a* difference. Two-tailed hypotheses are useful when it is hard to make a prediction. A two-tailed hypothesis for the sample experiment might be "Girls learning new math material in groups and girls learning new math material alone will perform differently on the XYZ math test."

Regardless of whether a researcher uses a one- or two-tailed hypothesis, it is crucial that the hypothesis contain **operationally defined variables:** the IV and the DV must be stated in clear and well-defined behavioral terms. Experiments are designed for **replication.** Researchers must be able to repeat the experiment to verify the original results.

I use a one-tailed hypothesis in the sample experiment.

Null Hypothesis

Experiments state a null hypothesis, which is the experimental hypothesis. A null hypothesis is a statement saying that there is little to no difference between the samples tested in the experiment (Coolican, 2004). The sample null hypothesis is "If the null hypothesis is true, there would be little difference between the scores on the XYZ math test between girls learning mathematics in groups and girls learning mathematics alone." It is best not to say that there will be no difference between the tested samples because a null hypothesis makes no specific prediction (Coolican, 2004).

The null hypothesis is the experimental hypothesis because all science experiments work according to probability. Researchers try to reject the null hypothesis within a reasonable margin of error. There is no proof that scientific theories are 100% true. The largest level of acceptable error in the social sciences is 5%. Inferential tests examine whether the null hypothesis can be rejected, not whether the research hypothesis is true.

The null hypothesis is *not* the opposite of the experimental hypothesis.

Method

The method section of experimental reports addresses the following: design, participants, materials, and procedures.

Design

Note to IB Students

> The SL and HL marking rubrics for method design are identical. You must identify a design, justify it, and identify the IV and DV. In addition, include a statement about how the experiment meets ethical standards.

Experimental design refers to the way groups or conditions are compared. There are two designs students frequently use for simple experiments:

1. Independent samples (between-groups designs)
2. Repeated measures (within-groups designs)

Design is an art form, and there are many ways to construct any experiment. The best experiments creatively address concerns about control and data collection.

A description of the two designs follows this paragraph (Goodwin, 1998; McMillan & Schumacher, 1984). But first there are a few things you need to know about selecting a design. A design needs to be justified as the best one for the experiment. *Justification comes primarily from the control offered by each design.* Sometimes students are vague about justifying the design. You must clearly use research design language about control in experiments. Each design controls specific **internal validity** concerns. A characteristic of experiments is the isolation of the IV from all extraneous variables. Internal validity refers to the control *within* an experiment. Just understand that selecting one design to control for threats to interval validity leaves other threats uncontrolled. There is no way to change this problem. Accept it as a limitation of experiments; there is no way to control for everything. The best you can do is control the internal validity threats that are the worst ones for your particular study.

1. **Independent samples.** Independent-samples designs compare two different groups. This is the best design for the sample math study because we want to investigate the effects of two different learning methods. *Independent-samples designs are justified as the best way to control for testing and progressive errors, order effects, maturation, and mortality.* However, independent-samples designs leave history uncontrolled.

2. **Repeated measures.** Repeated-measures designs compare the subject to himself or herself before and after the independent variable is introduced. This design could be used for the sample math experiment. One group of girls could be tested in the alone condition and then in the group condition. Repeated-measures designs work well for some experiments, such as those testing attitude change. However, the problem with testing errors is too great for the sample math study. *The main justification for selecting repeated-measures designs is to control history.* However, order effects, maturation, mortality, and testing are left uncontrolled.

You are now aware that different designs are selected to control threats to internal validity. Listed on the next page are 12 general **internal validity** concerns (Goodwin, 1998; McMillan & Schumacher, 1984), some of which are controlled by selecting either design. Internal validity refers to the control that a researcher applies to the study, such as making sure that participants do not have a chance to share information during the study. **The different designs offer control for varying aspects of these internal validity errors.** Decide which ones are most important and choose a design that maximizes the control of these threats. Because designs control only some things important to the study, *you may also have to put some control into your procedures.* It is impossible to control everything in an experiment. Sometimes one control choice causes another problem. For example, repeated-measures designs control for history but introduce order effects into experiments. Researchers should then control for order effects in their procedures by counterbalancing. Control issues are something all researchers face. Make the most justified choices to control as many variables as possible.

Some internal validity errors are **random errors.** Random errors are characteristics subjects bring with them to the study. Identifying and controlling random errors is not always possible. Controlling the sample and prescreening for subject variables that may **confound** the experiment as much as possible is recommended. **Systematic errors** are mistakes made by the researcher.

Random and systematic errors should be anticipated and accounted for before the experiment is run.

1. **History.** History refers to participant characteristics that negatively influence the experiment. Some random history errors always exist, even when control is attempted. Prescreening for unwanted subject variables is one action to take. There are going to be differences in prior math success regardless of what is found by prescreening the sample. These differences may relate to the participant's history of parental reinforcement, early childhood play, or experiences with teachers.

2. **Selection.** Selection is a systematic error and refers to sample bias. Researchers use random sampling to avoid selection bias. If opportunity sampling is used, make sure the participants are statistically equivalent and randomly allocated to the groups or conditions. Control the sample so that subject variables do not confound the study.

3. **Mortality.** Mortality is a systematic or a random error depending on the situation. Mortality refers to participants dropping out of the experiment before its completion (it does not mean dying!). It is a systematic error if the researcher makes the experiment too long or difficult for participants. It is a random error if the experiment is well designed with appropriate tasks but a participant leaves the study anyway. Participants have the ethical right to leave the study whenever they wish. Researchers may never know the reason.

4. **Maturation.** Maturation is a systematic or a random error depending on the situation. Maturation occurs when participants change after the study begins. Researchers avoid maturation errors by anticipating all potential possibilities. Experiments taking place over numerous days run the risk that a participant learns something new on the topic, such as information from a television documentary. Researchers cannot control every random instance of maturing. Maturation is best avoided by gathering all data at one time, a practice that is adequate for our simple study.

5. **Diffusion of treatment.** This systematic error occurs when participants share information about the study. Diffusion occurs in the sample math experiment if participants from each group have a chance to compare experiences outside the study before its completion. Two ways to control diffusion are to prevent participant interaction during the experiment and to collect data all at one time, such as within the 50-minute class period. Sometimes students want to design an experiment in which they compare memory after a short time, such as after 30 minutes, with memory after a long time, such as after a week. Waiting a week introduces the possibility of a diffusion-of-treatment error into the study, so you must decide

which is more important—seeing how memory works over time or controlling diffusion of treatment.

6. **Order effect.** Order effects are systematic errors in which the order of experimental tasks, rather than the IV, causes the responses of subjects. If an experiment involves showing participants a series of pictures, the participants tend to remember the first or the last one. **Counterbalancing** controls order effects. Half of the participants are shown the pictures in one order and the other half are shown the pictures in another order. Counterbalancing ensures that the experiment measures what it claims to measure. Repeated-measures designs should always use counterbalancing to avoid order effects.

7. **Hawthorne effect.** The Hawthorne effect occurs when participants alter their behavior simply to try to please the researcher by anticipating the correct answers. It is a systematic error if the researcher fails to consider how the Hawthorne effect influences the study. A **single-blind study**, where participants are deceived about the real nature of the study, controls the Hawthorne effect. However, the use of deception requires justification, and there are ways to control for the Hawthorne effect without deceiving participants. A **filler activity** is a good idea. At appropriate times, researchers distract participants with tasks having no relationship to the hypothesis. An example of a filler activity in a memory experiment is when participants read an article on another topic during the interval between the first exposure to words and the measurement of the DV in order to prevent rehearsal. In addition, researchers do not need to tell participants their exact hypothesis in order to obtain informed consent; they just tell them that it is a memory study, for example. Thus, participants are informed about the nature of the study, but the exact hypothesis has not been revealed.

8. **Experimenter bias.** A systematic error occurs when researcher behaviors influence participant behavior. **Demand characteristics** may exist, meaning that participants find out the true purpose of the study and think that certain behavior is "demanded" from them by the researcher. The researcher may not be aware that he or she is giving off subtle clues about the true nature of the study. Experimenter bias can be controlled. One way to control for experimenter bias is to use **standardized instructions**, which keeps researchers from accidentally adding anything to the predetermined instructions.

9. **Instrumentation.** Instrumentation is a systematic error leading to unanticipated changes in the results because of inconsistencies in data collection. In the sample experiment, the math material for the

two groups is exactly the same. Instrumentation can also occur when observation is used to collect data. If the observer becomes tired or there is a great deal happening at once, the checkmarks made on an observation grid may be inaccurate. Observing participants accurately is difficult and takes a lot of training.

10. **Constancy of condition.** Conditions must be the same for all participants; otherwise, a systematic error occurs. If the two groups of girls are tested in separate rooms, then conditions are not the same. **Balancing** controls this problem: half the girls in one group test in one room and half the same group test in another. The same thing occurs for the second group. Use the same testing area for all participants and conduct the experiment at one time to avoid constancy-of-condition errors. If one group is tested at 8:00 A.M. and the other at 1:00 P.M., there is also a constancy of condition error.

11. **Testing errors** and **progressive errors.** Both testing and progressive errors are systematic errors. Testing errors are the effects of pretesting on the posttest (the final measurement of the DV). Pretesting in independent-samples designs sometimes controls for history errors. However, the pretest may have an unwanted learning effect. Repeated-measures designs may contain testing errors. Progressive errors occur when participants practice the experimental skill before the experiment begins. Practice tests help make baseline skills equivalent, such as allowing participants practice at putting together a difficult puzzle. Practice tests control history but create a progressive error.

This is a long but important list. If an experiment has poor internal validity, the chances of **external validity** are small. External validity is to the extent to which the results of the study can be generalized outside the study. There are two types of external validity: **population validity** and **ecological validity.**

Population validity refers to generalizing the results to a larger population. It is limited to people from a target population with the same characteristics as those in the sample. Samples must be controlled so that researchers can say it was the IV that caused the changes in the DV. Uncontrolled samples might introduce history errors into the study.

Ecological validity involves generalizing based on experimental conditions, such as time of day, temperature, and the setting. If the experiment is run in a well-lighted, soundproof room at 9:00 A.M., this is the extent of its ecological validity. The conditions are very artificial, but researchers know that lab conditions are necessary to test the effects of an IV on a DV.

An independent-samples design is best for the sample math experiment. The testing error from the first trial still exists after counterbalancing in a repeated-measures design. History random errors are less threatening to the validity of the experiment. Subject variables are controllable in other ways, such as in the selection of research participants. Variables in the history of individual participants can **confound** the experiment. This means that characteristics of participants that are not measured in the experiment, such as prior learning or differences in intellectual level, might interfere with measuring the change in the DV. Confounding variables are easily controlled by selecting a controlled sample (see the section on participants).

The math experiment controls for subject variables in sample selection. The subject variables follow:

1. Math level. Choosing only honors-level trigonometry math students controls this variable.

2. Number of math courses taken. Selecting students in honors-level trigonometry with approximately equal numbers of courses in their histories controls this variable.

3. Sports history. Girls with a history of playing sports may have an advantage on spatial skills. Control is achieved by selecting students with approximately the same sports background.

4. Age. All subjects are 16 years old.

5. Cultural expectations. Different cultures may have different performance expectations, different efficacy levels for performance because culture affects efficacy, or different ways of problem solving or using memory. The experiment is limited to one culture.

6. Attribution style, or what people say is responsible for a success or failure. Girls generally have more internal attributions than males, blaming themselves for failure rather than an outside factor. It is safe to assume that attribution style is fairly constant among all girls.

7. Efficacy level, or the belief in one's ability to master a skill. Albert Bandura (1997) thinks math efficacy in girls can come from adult female models, among other things. Efficacy levels are difficult to examine in experiments because of ethical considerations. Separating girls by efficacy level raises the ethical risk of harming their self-esteem. This experiment does not control for efficacy differences. It adds a history risk, but the results can be triangulated with other methods.

The last thing needing attention in this section of the experiment report is a consideration of ethics.

Ethics in Experiments

All participants must give written, informed consent before participation and, if under 16, should have parental consent. A specific concern in the math experiment is protecting girls from potential harm to self-esteem, since girls may be "at risk" for low math efficacy. I designed the sample experiment to minimize this risk; the experiment has potential benefits, such as learning new study strategies. No situation should arise where subjects feel less competent because of the experimental tasks.

All student researchers should write a **briefing statement** that orients participants to the nature of the study before their participation. Participants should hear a **debriefing statement** at the end of data gathering that includes what the researchers expected to find. Participants should have access to the results after statistical tests are applied.

The APA guidelines are available at www.apa.org. The book *Ethics in Research with Human Participants* by Bruce Sales and Susan Folkman (2000) provides some insightful discussion on topics that high school students often do not consider.

The ethical issues that come up in simple studies include but are not limited to the following concerns:

1. Participants must give their informed consent.
2. The use of deception must be justified.
3. There should be no potential harm to participants. I suggest that students leave potential harm to the professional researchers. Professionals must show that the scientific benefit of the study outweighs the rights of participants and must include more details about the potential harm in the informed consent form.
4. Participants are volunteers and have the right to withdraw from the study at any time or withdraw their data from experimental results.
5. Participants have the right to a briefing and debriefing statement and must have a way to find out their results.

I find that well-meaning high school students often propose experiments containing potentially damaging situations. For example, students enjoy studying aggression theory and often want to make it the focus of class projects. I do not allow my students to do so because of the potential risk to themselves and to participants. Deceptive studies are also potentially problematic and involve issues about dispensing with informed consent, so I also do not allow deception in any of the high school experiments. A student's first experience with designing an experiment should focus on understanding design, not managing complex topics or ethical situations.

I require my students to design experiments that have a specific benefit for participants.

Participants

Note to IB Students

> Most of the marking rubric for participants is the same as the HL rubric except that SL students do not identify a target population.

Experiment reports give details about characteristics of the sample and how the sample is selected. This is important information for evaluating or replicating the study.

The sample must be controlled and should be small (about 15–20 participants). *Students typically want to use samples that are too large and varied.* Control the sample as much as possible. It is easy to get participants all the same age, all of the same grade, all males or females (if needed, such as in studies about spatial abilities), and all of the same intellectual level. In addition, large samples run the risk of introducing **confounding variables** into the study.

The sample is a subset of the larger **target population** to which results are generalized. The target population should be clearly identified. The entire population of girls in honors-level trigonometry at a school may be used in the sample experiment. However, the statistical concepts of sampling make it unnecessary. The sample is a representative group of the population if the sample is selected using some form of random sampling (which most students are unable to do in the school setting). **Population validity** is limited to those in the larger population with the same characteristics as the sample. **Selection bias** is avoided by using proper techniques for representational sampling.

Chapter 2 reviewed the difference between representative and nonrepresentative sampling. If it is possible to acquire a random sample, then you have a sample that represents a larger target population. Otherwise, an opportunity sample is used even though it does not represent a larger target population in a strict statistical sense. If you use opportunity sampling, the opportunity sample is the target population for your study.

Students can get frustrated at this point. They want to select a sample that represents a large group so that they can generalize their results outside the experiment. Just remember that experiments—including the samples—are supposed to be tightly controlled. Any one experiment does not generalize well. But if an experiment is part of a larger body of research with similar conclusions, then the study has more chances for generalization. See the section on generalizing from experiments at the very end of Chapter 11 to read more about this important topic.

Simple random sampling is an easy way to obtain a representative sample. Random sampling means that *everyone in the population to which researchers wish to generalize has an equal opportunity of being in the sample.* Random sampling provides the researcher with a representative sample of a larger target population. To obtain a random sample from the eleventh-grade girls taking honors-level trigonometry, all the girls are asked to volunteer for the experiment. Suppose they all volunteer. There are two steps involved.

1. Assign each girl a number, from 1 to 20, for example.
2. Have a computer or a calculator generate random numbers. The first number generated might be 4. So girl number 4 is selected for one group. The next number may be 11. This girl is now selected, and so on.

Another form of random sampling is **stratified random sampling.** An experiment about learning with the target population of the entire student body of St. Petersburg High School may have a selection bias without a stratified sample. Stratified sampling ensures that students of all age groups, cultural groups, grade levels, and ability levels, as well as both genders, are represented in the sample according to the percentage the group represents. If twelfth graders represent 20% of St. Petersburg High School, then 20% of the sample should be seniors. I think it is too hard for high school students to use stratified random sampling, but you and they should know what it is.

Researchers use **opportunity sampling** when random sampling is impossible. Opportunity sampling is justified because students working within the confines of the school schedule have limited chances to acquire a random sample and must select participants based on the convenience and opportunity to use them, such as all the students in Mrs. Smith's fourth-period English class.

Regardless of how samples are selected, researchers should use **random allocation** to assign participants to the groups or conditions. Random allocation is a feature of lab experiments and helps to control selection bias. Random allocation means that *everyone in the sample has an equal chance of* *being in either condition or group.* Random allocation is conducted in the same way as random sampling.

An opportunity sample of 20 girls from an eleventh-grade honors-level trigonometry class is used in the experiment. They are all 16 years old and have about the same math ability.

Materials

Note to IB Students

> The SL and HL rubrics for this section are identical. However, HL students should use the concept level of measurement here (defined in Chapter 11). SL students are not officially required to know about level of measurement. However, SL students are required to do things that are easier if the concept is understood. For example, different descriptive statistics are appropriate for the different levels of measurement. In addition, you will know more about why you are selecting different kinds of materials.

Designing materials is the first task. A decision about how to measure the dependent variable comes next. It is very important to identify the **level of measurement** (defined in Chapter 11) for the study as it determines which materials are appropriate for measuring the dependent variable.

The level of measurement must be correct because everything done with the data collected (descriptive and inferential statistics) must match the level of measurement. *Level of measurement refers to how the data are collected.* Everything else in the experiment falls into place once the level of measurement is identified correctly.

The sample experiment uses two groups of materials. The first is materials for new trigonometry concepts. The materials must be relevant for the trigonometry course and new to all participants. The second group is the XYZ math test to measure the DV. The XYZ test has a sample of problems that represent all facets of the new material. The XYZ test must accurately measure the DV. The length of the XYZ test is based on how well it mirrors tests typically used in the course. Scoring procedures must be explained. One point is awarded for each correct answer. A copy of all materials is included in the appendix at the end of the experiment. Specific information on the details of material development and scoring is provided for replication purposes. These two groups of materials make sense for the sample experiment topic.

I select an ordinal level of measurement for the sample experiment. It may seem that an interval level of measurement is appropriate. But while I can rank my scores, I cannot be sure that the rankings represent specific intervals. One reason is that all the math problems on the test cannot be assumed to be equivalent. A related issue arises when students count the number of words recalled by participants. Although it appears to be an interval, it may not really *be* an interval. Students can rank the scores, but it cannot be assumed that all the words are of equal difficulty. Time is a better example of a real interval. See Chapter 11 for more discussion on level of measurement.

Pilot (meaning a test run on participants similar to the ones used in the real study) the materials on a group similar to the participants in the real study before you run the experiment to make sure the materials are appropriate.

There are many ways to design materials to collect data. A list of some major data collection methods opens the next section. The choice of materials to use to collect data should reflect the level of measurement of your study.

There is one last thing to consider about data collection. Researchers are concerned with designing materials and procedures that minimize the chances of making a **type II error,** or the chance that the hypothesis is correct but the study is unable to show it; inferential testing accepts the null hypothesis. Students can easily try to maximize the chance that the IV is causing the difference in the DV by making sure that what is different about the two groups or conditions is *very* different (Coolican, 2004). If you do not find significance with an inferential test and the study is well controlled, the reason might be that you did not create enough of a difference between the groups or conditions. My students often think that if there is no significance between groups or conditions, then the study should be run on a larger and more varied group. Student perceptions make it seem as if a larger and more varied sample is needed, but the problem is usually more likely to be that the difference between the groups or conditions was not sufficiently great.

Ideas for Designing Materials

There are a number of ways to gather data for experiments that are appropriate for high school students.

1. Time participants on a task.
2. Count how many items on which participants get the correct answer.

3. Ask participants a question that can be answered with yes or no (or something similar).

4. Observe participants. Many researchers collect experimental data with an observation grid. Make sure that items on the grid measure only the dependent variable. The grid contains items fitting the operational definitions for behaviors representing the DV. Look at the example of an observation grid in Chapter 7.

5. Construct a questionnaire. **Make sure you understand that "questionnaires" for experiments are not the same thing as the questionnaires and surveys used in nonexperimental research.** Questionnaires for experiments can be used in two ways. First, the questionnaire can contain the IV, such as in the Loftus (1975) experiments. Loftus changed one word in one question on each questionnaire, called the critical question. All the other questions were filler questions. Second, a question or questions can measure the DV, such as a Likert Scale measuring the degree of likability participants assigned after reading different adjectives to describe a job candidate. Make sure that all questions on the instrument measure the dependent variable and nothing else. Follow these guidelines for writing good questions (McMillan & Schumacher, 1984). *All mistakes in question writing are instrumentation errors.*

   a. *Clearly state items.* There is a difference between a questionnaire asking general questions and one asking clear and specific questions. "I feel angry at my parents" is too general. Break it down into several questions containing specific behaviors, such as "My parents make fair rules about curfews."
   b. *Ask one question at a time.* Asking more than one item in a question is **double-barreled.** "Do you approve of the tardy policy and the dress code?" is double-barreled. If the subject answers yes, to which item is the subject responding? Break this question down into two separate questions.
   c. *Keep questions simple.* The longer and more complex a question, the greater the chance that it will be misunderstood or skipped.
   d. *Eliminate all negative questions.* Negative questions are misunderstood more than positive statements. Say "The cafeteria staff does a good job" rather than "The cafeteria staff is not doing a good job."
   e. *Edit the questions for biased language.* The Hawthorne effect is sometimes prompted by the way in which items are phrased. Gender-stereotyped language is an example. Sometimes students are not actively aware of cultural biases in language and should get advice on word choice. Slang is never appropriate.

Structured questionnaires use an accepted response format. Every question uses the same scale. There are four major types of such questions.

1. **Likert scales.** Likert scales rank-order responses. This format is used in experiments gathering data with ordinal levels of measurement. Here are two examples of scales:

    a. I approve of the dress code.

strongly agree	agree	neither agree or disagree	disagree	strongly disagree

    b. An appropriate dress code is:

critical	very important	important	somewhat unimportant	very unimportant

2. **Semantic differential scales.** This format uses adjective pairs. Subjects rate their opinions by marking somewhere on the scale between the opposing adjectives. Semantic differential scales are used with the ordinal level of measurement. Here are two examples:

    a. My parents are:
       fair _____ _____ _____ _____ _____ unfair
    b. My parents are:
       trusting _____ _____ _____ _____ _____ untrusting

    Make as many adjective pairs as necessary to measure the DV.

    There is a semantic differential scale for children. They fill in the happy, sad, or neutral face on the nose with crayon. If the children can read well, write very simple questions with the faces under each one. If the children cannot read well, say the question out loud and wait after each one for the children to fill in the nose.

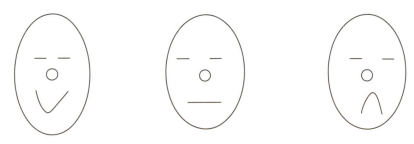

3. **Yes/no questions.** This format is for experiments using nominal levels of measurement. Yes/no formats do not supply much information about opinions. A response-style systematic error may exist

if a nominal scale is used in an experiment that is really appropriate for ordinal or interval levels of measurement.

4. **Checklists.** A checklist is appropriate for gathering data in experiments such as one on female career choices after an IV is introduced. Participants place a mark beside all of the relevant items on the checklist.

Procedures

The next part of this discussion is where you detail the procedures. Other researchers must be able to replicate the experiment. Procedures should be clear and precise. Be as specific as this example: "On the day of the experiment, the researcher went into Mrs. Smith's fourth-period eleventh-grade honors-level trigonometry math class. The researcher introduced himself to the class and informed potential participants of the nature of the experiment. Volunteers were obtained, randomly allocated," and so on.

Include any control features applied to your experiment that the design itself does not control. These are control features in the procedures that help make up for the threats to internal validity that the design left vulnerable. Here are two common examples: (1) If you selected a repeated-measures design, it is recommended that you counterbalance. (2) If you selected an independent-samples design, it is recommended that you screen participants for variables that might confound your study, such as an experiment on the Mozart effect screening out the few potential participants who are accomplished musicians. The procedures are also the place to control potential internal validity threats, such as diffusion of treatment. It is common for students to come up with a way to keep participants from talking to each other during the experiment. Since this is a big problem for students, make a clear plan on how to manage it.

Finally, describe how you applied ethical guidelines during the experiment. I suggest using a bullet list instead of writing about the procedures in a paragraph. Some of the bullets should clearly state when and how the ethical guidelines were applied. For example, if the first bullet is that you arrived in Mrs. Smith's fourth-period English class and introduced yourself, the second bullet might be that you informed the class that you were running a study on females and mathematics and wondered if anyone would be willing to volunteer. You are required to inform participants of the nature of the study and to make it clear that participation is not required. Integrate how you met ethical requirements throughout the procedures.

Analyzing Data from an Experiment

Some Context for Thinking about Data Analysis

This chapter includes important information about selecting appropriate descriptive and inferential statistics for analyzing raw data. The material is limited to analyzing simple experiments where one independent variable (IV) is manipulated and one dependent variable (DV) is measured. This book does not demonstrate calculations or discuss the statistical analysis for experiments manipulating more than one IV and/or measuring more than one DV. Calculations for descriptive and inferential statistics are easily accessed on the Internet or are available in texts such as Coolican (2004) or Runyon, Haber, Pittenger, and Coleman (1996).

Raw data are the data collected on subjects during the experiment. This is the score given to each participant representing the dependent variable, such as the number of items recalled or the number of math problems solved. Each participant gets an overall raw score.

On the next page is a chart representing raw data for the sample experiment. This chart should appear in the appendix of a research report; *it should never appear in the body of the report*. The raw data are used only to figure relevant descriptive and inferential statistics.

Raw data mean little until they are interpreted. It is necessary to know the **level of measurement** of the data before descriptive and inferential statistics are applied. The level of measurement guides decisions about selecting appropriate descriptive and inferential statistics. These guidelines are easy to learn and apply.

Number of Math Problems Completed Either Alone or in a Group			
Alone	Condition	Group	Condition
Subject 1	5	Subject 11	12
Subject 2	3	Subject 12	8
Subject 3	8	Subject 13	8
Subject 4	7	Subject 14	13
Subject 5	2	Subject 15	14
Subject 6	3	Subject 16	12
Subject 7	8	Subject 17	13
Subject 8	4	Subject 18	12
Subject 9	4	Subject 19	11
Subject 10	5	Subject 20	11

The level of measurement refers to how the data are collected. **Choosing a level of measurement is fundamentally a decision about how to measure the DV, something that all experimenters must consider.** The process of developing materials, collecting data, and analyzing data flows smoothly once you understand level of measurement. Level of measurement is the first thing I consider when designing an experiment. Most topics can be studied at any of the levels of measurement. Use the one that best fits what you want to know about behavior.

Sometimes students think they can tell a study's level of measurement by looking at a chart or seeing if numbers are used. Both ideas are incorrect. The reasoning is faulty and based on appearances. All experiments quantify data (use numbers to represent human characteristics).

Note to IB Students

While SL students are not required to study level of measurement, knowing about it will help you understand how to select the most appropriate measures of central tendency and dispersion.

Level of Measurement

The four levels of measurement are **nominal, ordinal, interval,** and **ratio** (Coolican, 2004; Goodwin, 1998; McMillan & Schumacher, 1984). The first two are **nonparametric** (are not normally distributed and do not fall on a bell curve). The last two are **parametric** (are normally distributed and fall on a bell curve). The best way to identify the level of measurement is to ask: "How did I collect data?"

1 **Nominal data.** Nominal data are the most crude of all the measurements and give the researcher the least amount of information about subjects. Nominal data are collected in mutually exclusive categories. The categories do not overlap and cannot be ranked. Asking for yes/no responses and categorizing subjects by hair color groups of blond, brunette, or redhead are examples. The Loftus (1975) eyewitness testimony experiment where participants were asked if they saw a barn is an example of a nominal-level experiment (participants answered yes or no).

2 **Ordinal data.** Ordinal data are also considered crude, but they give the researcher more information than nominal data do. Ordinal data are collected in such a way that they are ranked, and the rankings may overlap (are not mutually exclusive). Most human characteristics are ordinal. **Likert Scales** ranking subjects from the most to the least cooperative or the most to the least aggressive are ordinal scales. There may be some overlap between subject ratings, such as very aggressive and somewhat aggressive. The overlap is unknown. Ordinal scales are not designed to pick up small differences between responses, which is why they are considered crude. Ordinal data are collected in numbers artificially applied to human behaviors, such as 5 points for a very aggressive act.

There is no inherent meaning to the numbers assigned to nominal or ordinal scales; the numbers simply identify separations in the groups. Ordinal scales are not as precise as parametric scales, and they are not normally distributed. A *normal curve* is a theoretical curve standardizing scores. A normal distribution is not assumed for cooperation, creativity, or any other data examining a nonstandardized rating of human behavior. Most HS student experiments are at the ordinal level.

Nominal and ordinal levels of measurement are nonparametric. They are different from parametric levels of measurement, which must meet certain requirements. Theoretically, parametric levels of measurement are viewed as falling on a normal distribution, and data must be collected by interval or ratio levels of measurement. Nonparametric statistics allow researchers to have very small groups of subjects, use levels of measurement that are simple rankings or exclusive categories, and do not require data to fall on a normal distribution.

3 **Interval data.** Interval scales rank data, and the exact differences between the rankings are known. Interval scales are things such as the time it takes to complete a task and standardized measurements such as SAT scores. *The numbers are not arbitrarily assigned.* Interval levels of measurement for human characteristics require that the characteristics be standardized (converted into a score that falls into percentile rankings on a normal curve) or require data to be collected in naturally occurring intervals, such as time. Interval data are sometimes removed from everyday life. For example, many students resent having their achievement quantified as an SAT score. The score does not represent everything involved in achievement, but it is how a group of individuals decided to standardize it for universal interpretation purposes. IQ scores raise similar issues. Interval scales differ from ratio scales regarding the use of the 0 point on the scale. For example, temperature is an interval measurement; the 0 is a changing point rather than an absence of temperature (Goodwin, 1998). *Sometimes it is hard for students to tell the difference between interval and ordinal levels of measurement.* If you are not sure, treat the data as ordinal. For example, is the number of words recalled really an interval? Is it possible that the words are not equivalent? This means that some words may be easier to recall than others. If the words are not equivalent and some might be easier to remember than others, then treat the data as ordinal. For example, are some words easier for females or males to remember? This way you do not make a mistake in applying statistical tests for interval data that assume a normal distribution.

4 **Ratio data.** Ratio data take interval data one step further. Ratio data are expressed as a ratio, meaning that one measurement in a category—such as weight—can be twice as large as another measurement in that category. The 0 in ratio data represents a true zero point (Goodwin, 1998), an absence of something. Zero weight or length means the absence of weight or length. Because of the way in which ratio data use a "real" 0 point, they are the only data that are really expressed as a ratio. For example, 4 pounds is twice as heavy as 2 pounds, but 40°C is not twice as warm as 20°C—it is just warmer (because 0°C does not indicate the absence of temperature). Subjects are not typically weighed in the social sciences; psychologists tend to collect data in terms of the degree of the behavior (ordinal scales). Ratio data are used most often in the natural sciences.

Why care about levels of measurement? It sounds very dull, but it is important. All social and natural science experiments *require the researcher to make a choice about how to represent the DV.* The choice of measurement level is important for **ecological validity,** the **generalization** of the results outside experimental conditions. An experiment on human intelligence requires a decision about how to operationalize (make concrete and specific so it can be measured) the concept "intelligence." The word *intelligence* does not have only one meaning, though this is contrary to everyday experiences with the concept. The problem is that human characteristics do not always fall neatly into intervals or ratios. Researchers using ordinal scales of "intelligence" collect data in degrees, such as from "very innovative" to "not innovative." Researchers are free to define intelligence or any other characteristic in many different ways. Howard Gardner (1993) is a psychologist who devised a nonstandardized way of viewing intelligence. It is hard to quantify Gardner's seven intelligences, but they may be more ecologically valid. Data collected in intervals require standardized "intelligence," such as an IQ score (fits on a normal distribution). IQ generally represents *g,* an innate ability. IQ scores are easily quantified, but many researchers question their ecological validity. Generalizing the concept is limited to the operational definitions of "intelligence." Intelligence theory is a very controversial field. Knowing how intelligence is made operational helps the reader understand the strengths and weaknesses of the research.

Studies measuring the DV with an interval such as time also contain limitations. The time it takes to complete a task is just a small part of a total behavior.

Choose the best level of measurement for your research goals. Level of measurement is the first thing I consider when thinking about designing an experiment.

What is the level of measurement of the sample experiment? The DV is measured as the number of math problems solved, which appears to be an interval scale. However, consider whether the interval scale is a true interval scale. It may be more appropriate to think about the collected data as ordinal. Why? Many interval scales are arbitrary. GPA is an example. Grades vary from teacher to teacher, though the 4.0 scale seems uniform. Time and temperature are examples of truer interval scales. They are not made-up scales. The sample experiment really examines learning style. Data are collected as the number of math problems solved, and trigonometry covers a variety of material. Each teacher selects different problems for different tests. I had the option in the sample study to have participants rate their learning experience on an ordinal scale from "learning a great deal" to "learning a little." I selected the number of math problems solved. Either is appropriate, but each gives us a different interpretation of learning.

Results

The results section includes descriptive and inferential statistics. It is my task to explain in a short amount of space *why* certain descriptive and inferential statistics are used in data analysis so you will choose the best ones. Calculations are the easy part; formulas are easily accessed on the Internet or from Coolican (2004) or Runyon and colleagues (1996).

Descriptive Statistics

Note to IB Students

> Both SL and HL students are directed to select *one* measure of central tendency and *one* measure of dispersion, each of which should be the most appropriate for the study. Include a graph of the measure of central tendency.

After raw data are collected, researchers make choices about describing data in a way that makes sense to others. Descriptive statistics organize the raw data and are useful tools in the beginning stages of organizing and interpreting data. However, descriptive statistics cannot tell you whether or not to reject a null hypothesis. An apparently large difference in the scores of the two groups shows *a* difference, not necessarily a significant one.

Students are frequently apprehensive about statistics. But statistics are the easy part; the real challenge is designing a well-controlled study. The experiment's level of measurement guides the choices for descriptive statistics. It is unnecessary and inappropriate to simply calculate all available descriptive statistics. Each measure of central tendency and dispersion has a specific purpose, and you should use the one that best represents your data.

Students should report a relevant **measure of central tendency.** Measures of central tendency show the central point of a data set. Choose the **mean, median,** or **mode** depending on your level of measurement. All three are averages, so be careful not to use the word *average* in a general way. *The mean is best for interval data, the median for ordinal data, and the mode for nominal data.* When students use all three, I know they do not understand the purpose of each one. *Littering the results section with irrelevant statistics is incorrect.*

The mean is the sum of all scores in a data set divided by the number of scores. It is easily affected by extreme scores (outliers).

The median is the midpoint and is not affected by extreme scores.

The mode is the most frequently occurring score. Think of the mode this way: It is the number of people who said yes or said no or fall into some other category. Most of the nominal data experiments my students run contain more than one measure. For example, group A might have eight people who said yes and six people who said no. Group B might have ten people who said yes and four people who said no. The graph shows the yes and no responses from both groups (four bars).

Students should use a graphs representing the appropriate descriptive statistic, such as a bar graph of the median or mean. Graphing should not include raw data.

Report a **measure of dispersion** if it is appropriate for your level of measurement. Measures of dispersion show "the degree to which individual scores differ from one another in a data set" (Runyon et al., 1996, p. 142).

Experiments using nominal levels of measurement have no measure of dispersion because data are collected in categories, such as the number of people saying yes or no. Measures of dispersion are useful for experiments using ordinal, interval, and ratio levels of measurement.

The **range**, meaning the distance between the lowest and highest score, is limited because it is easily affected by extreme scores. Just one extreme score can distort the range (Runyon et al., 1996).

The **interquartile range** and the **semi-interquartile range** are better choices (are more stable than the range) for ordinal levels of measurement because they are not distorted by extreme scores. The interquartile range is the range of the middle 50% of scores. The semi-interquartile range is half of the interquartile range. Even if a distribution is skewed (**skew** refers to whether the distribution is symmetrical), the middle 50% of scores will fall into the semi-interquartile range (Runyon et al., 1996).

Standard deviation is meant for normally distributed data and is best for interval or ratio levels of measurement. The standard deviation represents the "average deviation between the mean and the observed score" (Runyon et al., 1996, p. 148) and is the square root of the **variance** (or how dispersed scores are from the mean). Accurate use of the mean and the standard deviation requires that data fall on a normal distribution.

Following is a chart summarizing how to select measures of central tendency and measures of dispersion. If you find the concept of level of measurement hard to understand, just follow the chart.

Level of measurement	Measure of central tendency	Measure of dispersion
Nominal	Mode	N/A
Ordinal	Median	Interquartile range and semi-interquartile range
Interval	Mean	Variance and standard deviation
Ratio	Mean	Variance and standard deviation

Experiment reports include a written summary of descriptive statistics. Experiment reports also include a **graph** of descriptive statistics. Create a simple bar graph showing the central tendency. For example, it might depict the median of each group.

Inferential Statistics

Note to IB Students

Inferential testing is only for HL students. Justify your use of an inferential test. Justification comes from the level of measurement and design. Students wanting to use a *t* test must do more to justify its use. There are three extra requirements outlined below (in addition to the design and level of measurement).

Inferential statistics go beyond describing data. They tell us whether there is a **significant difference** between the groups or conditions. A noticeable difference between the medians or means of two groups or conditions does not automatically imply that the difference is significant.

An inferential statistics test is the only way to know if a **null hypothesis** can be rejected. Students are interested in whether their hypotheses are correct or not, but there is really no direct way to test them. Instead, inferential statistics test null hypotheses. It may seem strange, but we must assume that the groups or conditions are very similar (what a null hypothesis says) unless we can show (through an inferential test) that they are not. Even if you reject the null hypothesis, *it does not prove that the research hy-*

pothesis is correct. This is consistent with the reality of **probability.** There are random errors in all social science experiments. It is impossible to be 100% sure that the independent variable (IV) caused change in the dependent variable (DV). Errors are part of all experiments to some degree. Errors might be related to the history of participants. Different learning styles *probably* caused the change in the independent variable in the sample experiment. It is impossible to *prove* that learning styles caused the change.

After calculating an inferential test, you get a **level of significance.** A level of significance is the probability that it was the independent variable, not chance, that caused the change in the dependent variable. Social science research allows a maximum of 5% error for experiments. Significance levels are reported, for example, as $p < .05$, representing 5% error, or $p < .01$, representing 1% error.

While there are many inferential tests, the chart below the tests that are best for the types of designs and levels of measurement in experiments manipulating one IV and measuring one DV. Experiment reports include a written summary of inferential test results.

Level of measurement	Independent samples	Repeated measures or matched pairs
Nominal	Chi square	N/A
Ordinal	Mann-Whitney U	Wilcoxon
Interval/Ratio	t test for independent groups (unrelated t test)	t test for dependent groups (related t test)

Students think that inferential statistics are difficult. But these tests are easy to select and calculate. The choice for an inferential test is determined by the design and level of measurement. Students already have experience using formulas. Some inferential tests can be calculated without a formula, requiring only that the data can be ranked and counted. The most difficult part of running an experiment is the design. Once the design is solid, everything falls into place behind it.

The sample experiment uses the Mann-Whitney U test. It is the best choice for small groups of subjects, and there is no assumption of a normal distribution. The Mann-Whitney U is also appropriate for independent-samples designs using an ordinal level of measurement. It is a systematic error to choose incorrect statistical tests. Why do I choose the Mann-Whitney U test over the unrelated t test? It has to do with my ultimate choice for level of measurement. This is why it is so important to understand level of measurement and get it right. The choice of an inferential test is easy after you are sure of how you want to define the level of measurement.

If you want to use a *t* test, make sure not to violate any of its assumptions. There is an extra step to complete before calculating a *t* test. Data must meet three requirements (Coolican, 2004), shown in the following list. If the data do not meet the requirements, go down to an ordinal-level test. Using the *t* test inappropriately is an error on the researcher's part, and the conclusions may be incorrect.

1. Data are really at the interval level of measurement.

2. Data are from a normal distribution. For example, if there are extreme scores, then the data are skewed and are unlikely to be normally distributed.

3. Check for the homogeneity of variance—that the variance (meaning differences or inconsistencies) in different samples from a population is similar. This step is only necessary in experiments using an independent-samples design. Coolican (2004) writes that the homogeneity of variance has the most chance of being a problem if the number of participants in the two groups is very different, such as 5 in one group and 20 in another. Usually my students randomly allocate volunteers evenly to groups, so this third requirement is typically not a problem. One way to see if your data meet this requirement is what Coolican (2004) refers to as a "rough guide," where "one variance is more than four times the value of the other (for small N, i.e., 10 or fewer) or more than twice the value for larger N" (p. 262). Using this rough guide keeps students from going through lengthy statistical calculations.

Discussion

Note to IB Students

The SL and HL requirements have some similarities and some differences. Both SL and HL students must have a well-developed discussion of descriptive and inferential statistics that analyzes the study results. SL students must discuss their results in relation to the replicated study; HL students must discuss their results in relation to the studies in the literature review. Both SL and HL students must provide an in-depth discussion of the strengths and limitations of the design and procedures and suggest appropriate modifications for future research.

All researchers offer critiques of studies in a discussion. There are numerous relevant critiques for the sample experiment. After running my pretend data through a ranking and counting method from Siegel (1956), I find a significance level of $p < .001$. This means that only 1 in 1000 times would chance have caused the change in the dependent variable rather than the independent variable manipulated by the researcher.

Below are some topics that should be addressed in the discussion section. In the first three, I provide an example of things I might say in the discussion about my findings in the sample experiment (in quotation marks).

1. "My results are consistent with the existing body of research on gender differences in mathematics education." Students are expected to relate their findings to the reviewed literature. Are your findings similar to or different from the reviewed studies? If different, why do you think you found something dissimilar? This is a good place to analyze the descriptive and inferential statistics.

2. "Even with a significance level of .001, there is still a small probability that chance caused the change in the dependent variable. These may be due to random participant variables." This means that characteristics of a person that make him or her different from another person can confound the study. There are many small differences among participants that are hard to screen for before the experiment, such as temperament or prior learning.

3. "The results cannot be generalized outside the opportunity sample because it is a nonrepresentative sample." Since generalization is a difficult concept, a separate section about generalizing from experiments follows this section. It should help you think of relevant things to say about the meaning of experiment results.

4. Did you leave any subject variables uncontrolled? One subject variable left uncontrolled in the sample study is self-efficacy level. It is possible that girls with low efficacy levels learn differently than those with high efficacy levels. Ethical concerns make it difficult to separate girls based on efficacy level or to test efficacy level after the introduction of an IV. However, it is a potential issue in studying this topic and should be researched in the future.

5. Are there any problems with the design of the experiment? Any design has strengths and limitations. Researchers choose a design because it offers them the most control, noting that the design leaves other things uncontrolled. It is hoped that the researcher's procedures address any weaknesses. For example, a repeated-measures

design controls for history, but it adds a potential order effect. A careful researcher counterbalances to reduce chances of order effects. Research design is an art form, and it is impossible to design an experiment that controls everything. For example, the sample study does not fully control for history. Go back and consider the list of 12 threats to interval validity in Chapter 10.

6. If there is not a significant difference between the two groups or conditions and the null hypothesis cannot be rejected, it is likely that there have been design mistakes (type II errors). It is unlikely that the sample is at fault (if the sample was well controlled). Perhaps what was different about the two groups or conditions was not different enough. In addition, you might not have controlled everything that needed controlling, such as diffusion of treatment. Suggesting that a larger sample be used in future research will not necessarily correct the problem. Instead, large and varied samples can introduce unwanted confounding variables into the study.

Generalizing from Experiments

Because generalization is a difficult but important concept, following is a summary list of points to consider as you examine the meaning of an experiment's results:

1. Students frequently overgeneralize the results of experiments.

2. Students must accept that any single experiment has limited generalizability.

3. Generalization is affected by the conditions of the study (ecological validity), the characteristics of the sample (population validity), and the way the independent and dependent variables are operationalized.

4. The ecological validity of experiments is typically low because experiments are artificial. Experiments test theories, not the real world. Artificiality is not really a valid criticism of experiments. Be wary of criticizing a study for doing what it is supposed to do.

5. An experiment is the only method that tests cause and effect. In order to see if one variable (the IV) causes another (the DV) to

change, all the other variables that might affect the DV must be controlled.

6. Control is a great strength of experiments. If an experiment is not well controlled (has poor internal validity), it will *never* have any external validity. A good source on this topic is Bandura (1973), especially the beginning of Chapter 3, which contains an informative (and funny) discussion about the purpose of experiments. Since most introductory psychology students study the Bobo experiments on aggression, this information is helpful in understanding Bandura's research goals and why experiments are useful.

7. The population validity of experiments is also generally low. Samples must be tightly controlled to make sure that subject variables do not confound the study. Since many experiments use opportunity samples, we cannot be sure that they represent a larger target population. Nonrepresentative samples *may* represent a larger population, but it is not certain that they do. In a strictly statistical sense, only samples selected through representative sampling actually represent a larger target population. However, these target populations are usually pretty narrow, as it is difficult to get a sample that represents a very large group.

8. It is important to understand how the IV and the DV are defined (operationalized). Any generalization outside the study is limited to situations with the same definitions.

9. Researchers realize that experiments are artificial and use controlled samples. They are not making errors when they create artificial research situations.

So, then, what conclusions can we draw about experiments?

10. It is inappropriate to make too many generalizations on the basis of one experiment.

11. Instead, experiments should be replicated by others using different samples. If the results are similar, then we can make more generalizations. Is the experiment part of a larger body of research that points in the same direction? Observer and method triangulation are important concepts. Perhaps independent researchers replicate the experiment and find the same thing (**observer triangulation**). Perhaps independent researchers design studies using other research methods, sometimes following successful experiments, and find the same thing

(**method triangulation**). Triangulation takes care of the limitations of any single experiment.

12. Ultimately, researchers hope to generalize their findings; constructing theories that explain behavior is the whole point of conducting psychological research. But the primary aim of experiments is to see if the theory is sound.

13. A good way to evaluate a single study is to ask, "Is the experiment well controlled?" It is not appropriate to evaluate an experiment by suggesting that it have greater ecological or population validity. In effect, you are then suggesting that the experiment become uncontrolled, defeating the purpose of experiments.

Appendix 1
Ideas for Student Experiments

I recommend that all students in an introductory course conduct a classic lab experiment. This is the best way to learn about the strengths and limitations of experiments.

Note to IB Students

> The following experiments are appropriate for the internal assessment project as long as the student manipulates an independent variable (IV).

The original studies listed here provide good ideas for student experiments. Please note that most published studies are pretty complex and often have more than one IV and DV.

How should students handle these complicated studies? I recommend that you select one IV and one DV from the original study and conduct a partial replication. A student's first experience with conducting controlled laboratory research should be simple. The point is for students to learn about setting up a valid experiment, not to create new knowledge.

Google the titles that are not from JSTOR; they are free (at the time of writing the book). I include some sources from JSTOR because some teachers have access to that database.

If these original articles are too difficult, some experiments are described in enough detail in texts. Any specialty cognitive psychology text is appropriate. Most introductory texts do not contain enough information for replicating an experiment.

If you come across an experiment while reading a text that you want to use, look it up in the references or Google the title. You might be surprised at how many are free.

I do not allow my students to use any type of deception in experiments. Instead, look for ways to improve a skill. This way there is a benefit for participants and there is less chance that they will feel duped by being in the study.

1. **Eyewitness testimony:** Free on the Internet

    Loftus, E. F. (1975). Leading questions and the eyewitness report. *Cognitive Psychology, 7,* 550–572.

    Chambers, K. L., & Zaragoza, M. S. (2001). Intended and unintended effects of explicit warnings on eyewitness suggestibility: Evidence from source identification tests. *Memory and Cognition, 29*(8), 1120–1129.

2. **Mozart effect:** Google "Frances Rauscher" to get to her website, which provides a list of many studies. One that describes the original study follows; it is free on the Internet.

    Rauscher, F. H., Shaw, G. L., & Ky, K.N., (1993). Music and spatial task performance. *Nature, 365,* 611.

3. **Memory:** Free on the Internet

    Stroop, J. R. (1935). Studies of interference in serial verbal reactions. *Journal of Experimental Psychology, 18,* 643–662. Available from the website Classics in the History of Psychology.

    MacLeod, C. M. (1991). Half a century of research on the Stroop effect: An integrative review. *Psychological Bulletin, 109*(2), 163–203.

    Gao, Q., Chen, Z., & Russell, P. (2007). Working memory load and the Stroop interference effect. *New Zealand Journal of Psychology, 36*(3), 146–153.

    Craik, F. I. M., & Tulving, E. (1975). Depth of processing and the retention of words in episodic memory. *Journal of Experimental Psychology, 104*(3), 268–294.

    Baddeley, A. D. (1966). Short-term memory for word sequences as a function of acoustic, semantic, and formal similarity. *Quarterly Journal of Experimental Psychology, 18,* 362–365.

    Sperling, G., & Speelman, R. G. (1970). Acoustic similarity and auditory short-term memory: Experiments and a model. In D. A. Norman (Ed.), *Models of human memory* (pp. 151–202). New York: Academic Press.

    Roediger, H. L. (1990). Implicit memory. *American Psychologist, 45*(9), 1043–1056.

    Tulving, E. (1962). Subjective organization in free recall of unrelated words. *Psychological Review, 69*(4), 344–354.

    Kahana, M. J., & Howard, M. W. (2005). Spacing and lag effects in free recall of pure lists. *Psychonomic Bulletin and Review, 12*(1), 159–164.

4. **Attention:** The first is available on JSTOR; the other two are free on the Internet.

Treisman, A., Viera, A., & Hayes, A. (1992). Automaticity and preattentive processing. *The American Journal of Psychology, 105*(2), 341–362.

Cavanagh, P., Arguin, M., & Treisman, A. (1990). Effect of surface medium on visual search for orientation and size features. *Journal of Experimental Psychology, 16*(3), 479–491.

Mulligan, N. W., & Hartman, M. (1996). Divided attention and indirect memory tests. *Memory & Cognition, 24*(4), 453–465.

5. **Perception:** The first is available on JSTOR; the second is free on the Internet.

Wiseman, S., & Neisser, U. (1974). Perceptual organization as a determinant of visual recognition memory. *American Journal of Psychology, 87*(4), 675–681.

Goolsby, B. A., & Suzuki, S. (2001). Understanding priming of color-singleton search: Roles of attention at encoding and "retrieval." *Perception & Psychophysics, 63*(6), 929–944.

6. **Problem solving:** Available on JSTOR

Fantino, E., Jaworski, B. A., Case, D. A., & Stolarz-Fantino, S. (2003). Rules and problem solving: Another look. *American Journal of Psychology, 116*(4), 613–632.

7. **Mental imagery:** Free on the Internet

Finke, R. A., Pinker, S., & Farah, M. J. (1989). Reinterpreting visual patterns in mental imagery. *Cognitive Science, 13*(3), 252–257

Appendix 2
Idea for an Observation Study

Structured observation studies are the easiest to run. One idea is to observe children's play. Students go to a public park, playground, or beach to collect data. An example of a research question is "To what extent do gender differences exist in children's play?" Students can make an observation grid in class that includes some important gender differences that might occur, along with columns for males and females. Make sure the terms are operationalized. Everyone in the class can use the same observation grid. I also suggest time sampling, where students make one mark per incidence over a two-hour period. Two hours of observation is enough. High-quality observation research is challenging, and it is easy to make instrumentation errors, for example, when the researcher gets tired or distracted and so misses some important behavior. Perhaps two or more students should observe the same group (not sitting together in order to reduce experimenter bias) and then compare observations. If the observations deviate substantially, then the study is flawed.

One way to analyze data is to use frequencies and then identify important themes about gender differences in children's play. Another way is to use descriptive statistics.

The class needs to consider all the important ethical considerations relevant to conducting observation research addressed in Chapter 3. In addition, when my students go somewhere to collect data, I first ask parents to sign a permission form saying they know where the student is at all times and approve of the observation site.

Appendix 3
Idea for a Student Case Study

This is an idea for a case study on children's stories, their understanding of cultural expectations, and their cognitive development. It is well documented that children use stories to understand the behaviors that their culture expects. I use this project along with a lesson about language as a cognitive process.

Here are two sources for background theory and research:

Bruner, J. (1990). *Acts of meaning*. Cambridge, MA: Harvard University Press.

Engel, S. (1995). *The stories children tell: Making sense of the narratives of childhood*. New York: W. H. Freeman.

A participant between the ages of 2 and 7 is required. The child must have enough language to participate in storytelling. Get written permission from a parent and also ask for the child's permission to record stories.

The goal is to record two or three stories. Younger children need lots of help. At age 2, a child needs an adult to take an active lead and then maintain the story. At age 7, the child should need little to no assistance. Children aged 3 to 6 need a balance between telling the story on their own and getting adult assistance. Play a game with the child to break the ice. Younger children may need to play the entire time.

Record the stories. I suggest verbatim transcription. This is time-consuming, but students will appreciate the effort that goes into data transcription!

Next, put the stories into Bruner's (1990) categories of iconic (the child has some language and thinks in images rather than symbolically) or symbolic phases (the child has full command of language and has internal abstract representations) of cognitive development. Some children are transitioning between the two phases. In this case, select the best category. Students do not work with children without language in this study, so no child will fall into the enactive phase.

Next, decide which stories meet Bruner's criteria for narratives, a special type of story that helps children understand cultural rules. Engel (1995) outlines Bruner's criteria for narratives. A narrative has the following characteristics:

1. The story has a sequence.
2. The story has a meaningful plot.
3. The story has a high point.
4. The story may or may not be true.
5. The child makes distinctions between commonplace and unusual events.
6. The child draws attention to (points out) his or her subjective experiences.

Last, identify and explain the main themes that emerge about the children's level of cognitive development and how stories have assisted them in understanding what is expected behavior in their culture.

Appendix 4
Ideas for Questionnaire Studies

Designing good questionnaires is challenging. I suggest that students select a narrow topic for a questionnaire. Focus on a topic that might help resolve a school issue, such as perceptions and preferences about class scheduling, student privileges, or course offerings. These topics can be applied to school-based decisions.

I recommend that students avoid topics that require others to disclose personal information, such as GPA or assessment of one's level of mental health.

Write about 10 to 15 questions. Ask a specific target population to fill out the questionnaires. Make sure that participants remain anonymous.

Students can analyze the data with percentages, measures of central tendency, and measures of dispersion. If data are collected on age or grade level, perhaps answers can be correlated to those factors.

References

Alexander, K. J., Miller, P. J., & Hengst, J. A. (2001). Young children's emotional attachments to stories. *Social Development, 10*(3), 374–398.

American Psychological Association (APA). (2002). Ethical principles of psychologists and code of conduct. Retrieved May 21, 2006, from apa.org/ethics/code2002.html

Anderson, C. A., & Bushman, B. J. (2002). Human aggression. *Annual Review of Psychology, 53,* 27–51.

Anderson, C. A., & Anderson, K. B. (1996). Violent crime rate studies in philosophical context: A destructive testing approach to heat and southern culture of violent effects. *Journal of Personality and Social Psychology, 70,* 740–756.

Arthur, S., & Nazroo, J. (2003). Designing fieldwork strategies and materials. In J. Ritchie & J. Lewis (Eds.), *Qualitative Research Practice.* London: Sage Publications.

Azar, B. (2000, April). Online experiments: Ethically foul or fair? *Monitor on Psychology, 31*(4). Retrieved June 16, 2006, from apa.org/monitor/apr00/fairorfoul.html

Babyak, M., Blumenthal, J. A., Herman, S., Khatri, P., Doraiswamy, M., Moore, K., Craighead, E., Baldewicz, T. T., & Krishnam, K. R. (2000). Exercise treatment for major depression: Maintenance of therapeutic benefit at 10 months. *Psychosomatic Medicine, 62,* 633–638. Retrieved March 11, 2008, from http://www.psychosomaticmedicine.org/cgi/reprint/62/5/633

Bandura, A. (1965). Influence of model's reinforcement contingencies on the acquisition of imitative responses. *Journal of Personality and Social Psychology, 1*(6), 589–595.

Bandura, A. (1973). *Aggression: A social learning analysis.* Englewood Cliffs, NJ: Prentice Hall.

Bandura, A. (1997). *Self-efficacy: The exercise of control.* New York: Worth.

Bandura, A., Ross, D., & Ross, S. (1963). Imitation of film-mediated aggressive models. *Journal of Abnormal and Social Psychology, 66*(1), 3–11.

Becker, A. E., Burwell, R. A., Gilman, S. E., Herzog, D. B., & Hamburg, P. (2002). Eating behaviors and attitudes following prolonged exposure to television among ethnic Fijian adolescent girls. *British Journal of Psychiatry, 180,* 509–514.

Caspi, A., Sugden, K., Moffitt, T. E., Taylor, A., Craig, I. W., Harrington, H., McClay, J., Mill, J., Martin, J., Braithwaite, A., & Poulton, R. (2003). Influence of life stress on depression: Moderation by a polymorphism in the 5-HTT gene. *Science, 301,* 386–389.

Chiao, J. Y., Harada, T., Komeda, H., Li, Z., Mano, Y., Saito, D., Parrish, T. B., Sadato, N., & Iiaka, T. (2009). Neural basis of individualistic and collectivistic views of self. *Human Brain Mapping, 30*(9), 1–8.

Christensen, L., & Burrows, R. (1990). Dietary treatment of depression. *Behavior Therapy, 21,* 183–193.

Cohen, A. B., Tenenbaum, G., & English, R. W. (2006). Emotions and golf performance: An IZOF-based applied sport psychology case study. *Behavior Modification, 30*(3), 259–280.

Cohen, L., Manion, L., & Morrison, H. (2000). *Research methods in education* (5th ed.). London: Routledge.

Coolican, H. (2004). *Introduction to research methods and statistics in psychology* (4th ed.). London: Hodder & Stoughton.

DeRubeis, R. J., Hollon, S. D., Amsterdam, J. D., Shelton, R. C., Young, P. R., Salomon, R. M., O'Reardon, J. P., Lovett, M. L., Gladis, M. M., Brown, L. L., & Gallop, R. (2005, April). Cognitive therapy vs. medications in the treatment of moderate to severe depression. *Archives of General Psychiatry, 62.* Retrieved March 12, 2008, from http://www.archgen psychiatry.com

Ehrmin, J. T. (2002). "That feeling of not feeling": Numbing the pain for substance abuse-dependent African American women. *Qualitative Health Research, 12,* 780–791.

Gardner, H. E. (1993). *Frames of mind: The theory of multiple intelligences.* New York: Basic Books.

Garner, D. M., & Garfinkel, P. E. (1979). The Eating Attitudes Test: An index of the symptoms of anorexia. *Psychological Medicine, 9,* 273–279.

Gillham, B. (2008). *Observation techniques: Structured to unstructured.* London: Continuum.

Goodwin, C. J. (1998). *Research in psychology: Methods and Design* (2nd ed.). New York: John Wiley & Sons.

Hanin, Y. L. (2003). Performance related emotional states in sport: A qualitative analysis. *Forum: Qualitative Social Research, 4*(1).

Hargreaves, D. A., & Tiggermann, M. (2006). Body image is for girls: A qualitative study of boy's body image. *Journal of Health Psychology, 11*(4), 567–576.

Hock, R. R. (2005). *Forty studies that changed psychology* (5th ed.). Upper Saddle River, NJ: Pearson.

Keller, M. B., McCullough, J. P., Klein, D. N., Arnow, B., Dunner, D. L., Gelenberg, A. J., Markowitz, J. C., Nemeroff, C. B., Russell, J. M., Thase, M. E., Trivedi, M. T., & Zajecka, J. (2008). A comparison of nefazodone, the cognitive-behavioral system of psychotherapy, and their combination for the treatment of chronic depression. *New England Journal of Medicine, 342,* 1462–1470. Retrieved October 28, 2008, rom http://www.nejm.com

Kimura, D., & Clarke, P. (2002). Women's advantage on verbal memory is not restricted to concrete words. *Psychological Record, 91,* 1137–1142. Retrieved March 16, 2005, from http://www.sfu.ca/~dkimura/

Legard, R., Keegan, J., & Ward, K. (2003). In-depth interviews. In J. Ritchie & J. Lewis (Eds.), *Qualitative research practice: A guide for social science students and researchers.* London: Sage Publications.

Lewis, J. (2003). Design issues. In J. Ritchie & J. Lewis (Eds.), *Qualitative research practice: A guide for social science students and researchers.* London: Sage Publications.

Lewis, J., & Ritchie, J. (2003). Generalizing from qualitative research. In J. Ritchie & J. Lewis (Eds.), *Qualitative research practice: A guide for social science students and researchers.* London: Sage Publications.

Loftus, E. F. (1975). Leading questions and the eyewitness report. *Cognitive Psychology, 7,* 550–572.

Ma, J. L. (2008). Eating disorders, parent-child conflicts, and family therapy in Shenzhen, China. *Qualitative Health Research, 18*(6), 803–810.

McMillan, J. & Schumacher, S. (1984). *Research in education.* Boston: Little, Brown.

National Institute of Mental Health (NIMH). (1997). The Diagnostic Interview Schedule (DIS-IV). Available from http://epi.wustl.edu/DIS/disdescription.htm.

Neuman, W. L. (2006). *Social research methods: Qualitative and quantitative approaches* (6th ed.). Boston: Pearson.

Nightingale, D. J., & Cromby, J. (1999). *Social constructionist psychology: A critical analysis of theory and practice.* Buckingham, UK: Open University Press.

Okello, E. S., & Musisi, S. (2006). Depression as a clan illness (eByekika): An indigenous model of psychotic depression among the Baganda of Uganda. *World Cultural Psychiatry Research Review, 1*(2), 60–73.

Petrova, P. K., Cialdini, R. B., & Sills, S. J. (2007). Consistency-based compliance across cultures. *Journal of Experimental Social Psychology, 43,* 104–111.

Ritchie, J. (2003). The applications of qualitative research. In J. Ritchie & J. Lewis (Eds.), *Qualitative research methods: A guide for social science students and researchers*. London: Sage Publications.

Ritchie, J., Lewis, J., & Elam, G. (2003). Designing and selecting samples. In J. Ritchie & J. Lewis (Eds.), *Qualitative research methods: A guide for social science students and researchers*. London: Sage Publications.

Ritsko, A., & Rawlence, C. (Directors). Secrets of the mind [Episode of TV series *Nova*]. Boston: WGBH.

Rosenhan, D. (1973). *On being sane in insane places*. Retrieved May 5, 2009, from http://web.coc.edu/lminorevans/on_being_sane_in_insane_places .htm

Rosenthal, R. (1993). *Homeless in paradise*. Philadelphia: Temple University Press.

Runyon, R. P., Haber, A., Pittenger, D. J., & Coleman, K. A. (1996). *Fundamentals of behavioral statistics* (8th ed.). New York: McGraw-Hill.

Sales, B. D., & Folkman, S. (2000). *Ethics in research with human participants*. Washington, DC: American Psychological Association.

Siegel, S. (1956). *Nonparametric statistics for the behavioral sciences*. New York: McGraw-Hill.

Singelis, T. (1999). Singelis Self-Construal Scale. Available from www. psychology.ucdavis.edu/acrdr/meausres/singelisscs.doc

Snape, D., & Spencer, L. (2003). The foundations of qualitative research. In J. Ritchie & J. Lewis (Eds), *Qualitative research practice: A guide for social science students and researchers*. London: Sage Publications.

Stanovich, K. E. (2007). *How to think straight about psychology* (8th ed.). New York: Longman.

Washington University in St. Louis. (n.d.). C DIS-IV description. Available at http://epi.wustl.edu/DIS/disdescription.htm

Willig, C. (2001). *Introducing qualitative research in psychology: Adventures in theory and method*. New York: Open University Press.

Wolfe, H. L. (2005). Acupuncture and depression. Retrieved August 31, 2008, from http://www.bluepoppy.com

World Health Organization. (2004). Prevalence, severity, and unmet needs for treatment of mental disorders in the World Health Organization world mental health surveys. *Journal of the American Medical Association, 291*(21). Retrieved October 8, 2008, from http://www.jama.com

Yin, R. (2009). *Case study research: Design and methods* (4th ed.). Los Angeles: Sage Publications.

Index

abstraction, levels of, 59
access ladder, 56–57
aim of study, statement of, 87
Alexander et al., "Young children's
    emotional attachments to
    stories"
    combined qualitative methods in, 8
    credibility of, 28
    detailed observations in, 55
    main description of study, 51–54
    researcher bias and, 28
    research question answered by, 4
analytical generalization
    case studies and, 68
    in Ma, "Eating disorders," 62–63
analytic memos, 58
Anderson and Anderson, "Violent
    crime rate studies," 81–82
anonymity
    overview, 18–19
    questionnaires and, 82
    Rosenhan study and, 51
archival records, 61
artificiality
    of laboratory experiments, 116,
    117
    of quantitative vs. qualitative data,
    5, 6
attitude of strangeness, 57

balancing, 95
Bandura Bobo doll experiments
    causation established by, 3, 6
    experimental control and, 117
    method triangulation and, 22
    observation checklists in, 45
    research questions answered by, 3
Beck Depression Inventory, 74
Becker et al., "Eating behaviors and
    attitudes"
    combined quantitative and
    qualitative methods in, 8
    correlation determined by, 6
    main descriptions of study, 34–35, 72

purposive sampling in, 13, 25
research question answered by, 3
between-group designs. *see*
    independent-samples designs
bias, researcher. *see* researcher bias
bias, selection. *see* selection bias
biased language, 102
Bobo doll experiments. *see* Bandura
    Bobo doll experiments
briefing statements, 97
Brooks, John, 81
Bruner, Jerome, 22

case studies
    advantages and disadvantages,
    66–67
    examples
        Cohen et al., "Emotions and golf
        performance" (*see* main entry
        under "Cohen")
        Ma, "Eating disorders" (*see* main
        entry under "Ma")
    generalizability of, 67–68
    ideas for, 123–124
    overview, 60–61
    research questions answered by, 4
    triangulation of qualitative research
    and, 30–31
Caspi et al., "Influence of life stress on
    depression"
    correlation determined by, 6
    main description of study, 73–74
    representative sampling in, 78
    research questions answered by, 3
categories, data
    formation of, in observational
    studies, 58–59
    inductive content analysis of, 43–44
    in Ma, "Eating disorders," 63
causation, establishing
    experimental studies and, 6,
    116–117
    method triangulation and, 22
    vs. correlation, 79, 81